Death of a Salesman

Arthur Miller

Death of a Salesman

Certain Private Conversations
in Two Acts and a Requiem

Text and Study Aids

Edited and annotated
by Peter Bruck
and Rudolph F. Rau

Ernst Klett Sprachen
Stuttgart

1. Auflage   1   17 16 15 14 13 | 2023 22 21 20 19

Alle Drucke dieser Auflage können im Unterricht nebeneinander
benutzt werden.
Death of a Salesman is reprinted by permission of International
Creative Management, Inc. Copyright © 1949, 1977 by Arthur Miller.
© für diese Ausgabe Ernst Klett Sprachen GmbH, Rotebühlstraße 77,
70178 Stuttgart, 2008.
Alle Rechte vorbehalten.
Internetadresse: www.klett-sprachen.de

Herausgegeben von Dr. Peter Bruck, Lüdinghausen (Textwahl, Fragen)
und Rudolph Franklin Rau, M. A., Weinstadt (Vorwort, Vokabular).
Fotos: Kinoarchiv Engelmaier (Umschlag); Ullstein Bilderdienst
(Autor)
Redaktion: Dr. Hartmut K. Selke
Druck: CPI – Ebner & Spiegel, Ulm
Printed in Germany.

ISBN 978-3-12-577633-3

9 783125 776333

CONTENTS

INTRODUCTION

Arthur Miller (1915 – 2005) was one of the most successful and enduring playwrights of the second half of the twentieth century in America, no doubt because his focusing on middle-class anxieties brought on by a society that emphasizes the hollow values of material success has struck such a responsive chord. The recurring theme of anxiety and insecurity reflects much of Arthur Miller's own past. Born the son of a well-to-do Jewish manufacturer in New York City in 1915, Miller had to experience the social disintegration of his family when his father's business failed during the Great Depression of the 1930s. By taking on such odd jobs as waiter, truck driver, and factory worker, Miller was able to complete his studies at the University of Michigan in 1938. These formative years gave Miller the chance to come in close contact with those who suffered the most from the Depression and instilled in him a strong sense of personal achievement necessary to rise above the situation. He began writing plays in the 1930s, but it wasn't until *Death of a Salesman* was performed in 1949 that Miller established himself as a major American dramatist.

Winning the Pulitzer Prize in 1949, *Death of a Salesman* has to this day remained a classic. The play's intellectual appeal lies in Miller's refusal to portray his characters as two-dimensional – his refusal to involve himself in a one-sided polemic attack on capitalism. Even critics cannot agree as to whether *Death of a Salesman* is to be categorized as social criticism, a tragedy, or simply a psychological study. Of necessity, each person will have to draw his or her own individual conclusions.

The fact that performances of *Death of a Salesman* have met with acclaim throughout the world testifies to its universality: the play's conflicts and themes appear not to be uniquely American.

THE CHARACTERS

WILLY LOMAN
LINDA
BIFF
HAPPY
BERNARD
THE WOMAN
CHARLEY
UNCLE BEN
HOWARD WAGNER
JENNY
STANLEY
MISS FORSYTHE
LETTA

The action takes place in Willy Loman's house and yard and in various places he visits in the New York and Boston of today.

New York premiere February 10, 1949.

ACT ONE

A melody is heard, played upon a flute. It is small and fine, telling of grass and trees and the horizon. The curtain rises.

  Before us is the Salesman's house. We are aware of towering, angular shapes behind it, surrounding it on all sides. Only the
5 *blue light of the sky falls upon the house and forestage; the surrounding area shows an angry glow of orange. As more light appears, we see a solid vault of apartment houses around the small, fragile-seeming home. An air of the dream clings to the place, a dream rising out of reality. The kitchen at center seems*
10 *actual enough, for there is a kitchen table with three chairs, and a refrigerator. But no other fixtures are seen. At the back of the kitchen there is a draped entrance, which leads to the living room. To the right of the kitchen, on a level raised two feet, is a bedroom furnished only with a brass bedstead and a straight chair. On a*
15 *shelf over the bed a silver athletic trophy stands. A window opens onto the apartment house at the side.*

  Behind the kitchen, on a level raised six and a half feet, is the boys' bedroom, at present barely visible. Two beds are dimly seen, and at the back of the room a dormer window. (This bedroom is
20 *above the unseen living room.) At the left a stairway curves up to it from the kitchen.*

  The entire setting is wholly or, in some places, partially transparent. The roof-line of the house is one-dimensional; under and over it we see the apartment buildings.

25 *Before the house lies an apron, curving beyond the forestage into the orchestra. This forward area serves as the back yard as well as the locale of all Willy's imaginings and of his city scenes. Whenever the action is in the present the actors observe the imaginary wall-lines, entering the house only through its door at*

---

3 **towering** very tall and impressive – 4 **angular shapes** shapes (of buildings) which seemingly spread apart as they rise – 5 **forestage** [ˈ‒ ‒] see glossary – 6 **glow** steady bright light such as produced by a setting sun – 7 **solid** with no gaps – 7 **vault** rounded ceiling often in a church, here used metaphorically – 8 **fragile** [ˈfrædʒaɪl] which can be easily broken or damaged – 8 **the dream** possibly Willy Loman's dream – 8 **to cling** to hold on tightly to sb or sth – 10 **actual** real – 11 **fixture** a piece of furniture or equipment that is fixed in a house, e.g. sink – 12 **draped** with a piece of cloth hanging over it – 14 **brass** Messing – 14 **bedstead** frame for a bed – 15 **trophy** [ˈtrəʊfi] – 18 **dimly** not easily seen because of being too dark – 19 **dormer window** an upright window built into a roof – 20 **to curve** to bend round – 22 **partially** not completely – 22 **transparent** [‒ˈ‒ ‒] which can be seen through – 25 **apron** the part of the stage in front of the curtain – 27 **locale** [ləʊˈkɑːl] scene, setting

the left. But in the scenes of the past these boundaries are broken, and characters enter or leave a room by stepping "through" a wall onto the forestage.

From the right, Willy Loman, the Salesman, enters, carrying
5 *two large sample cases. The flute plays on. He hears but is not aware of it. He is past sixty years of age, dressed quietly. Even as he crosses the stage to the doorway of the house, his exhaustion is apparent. He unlocks the door, comes into the kitchen, and thankfully lets his burden down, feeling the soreness of his*
10 *palms. A word-sigh escapes his lips – it might be "Oh, boy, oh, boy." He closes the door, then carries his cases out into the living room, through the draped kitchen doorway. Linda, his wife, has stirred in her bed at the right. She gets out and puts on a robe, listening. Most often jovial, she has developed an iron repression*
15 *of her exceptions to Willy's behavior – she more than loves him, she admires him, as though his mercurial nature, his temper, his massive dreams and little cruelties, served her only as sharp reminders of the turbulent longings within him, longings which she shares but lacks the temperament to utter and follow to their*
20 *end.*

LINDA *(hearing Willy outside the bedroom, calls with some trepidation)*: Willy!

WILLY: It's all right. I came back.

LINDA: Why? What happened? *(Slight pause.)* Did something
25 happen, Willy?

WILLY: No, nothing happened.

LINDA: You didn't smash the car, did you?

WILLY *(with casual irritation)*: I said nothing happened. Didn't you hear me?

30 LINDA: Don't you feel well?

---

5 **sample case** a suitcase containing examples of the articles for sale – 7 **exhaustion** state of being very tired – 9 **burden** heavy load – 9 **soreness** pain from overuse – 10 **palm** the inside of the hand without the fingers – 10 **a word-sigh** a word expressed as one lets out a deep breath when tired or disappointed – 13 **to stir** to move slightly – 13 **robe** kind of coat worn over nightclothes – 14 **jovial** [ˈdʒəʊvɪəl] cheerful – 14 **iron repression** great ability not to let feelings show – 15 **exception** objection, opposition – 16 **mercurial nature** [mɜːˈkjʊərɪəl] personality characterized by rapidly changing moods – 18 **turbulent** [ˈ– – –] restless, confused – 18 **longing** a desire for sth – 19 **to utter** to express in words – 21 **trepidation** fear – 28 **casual** showing little interest or concern – 28 **irritation** annoyance

WILLY: I'm tired to the death. *(The flute has faded away. He sits on the bed beside her, a little numb.)* I couldn't make it. I just couldn't make it, Linda.

LINDA *(very carefully, delicately)*: Where were you all day? You
5 look terrible.

WILLY: I got as far as a little above Yonkers. I stopped for a cup of coffee. Maybe it was the coffee.

LINDA: What?

WILLY *(after a pause)*: I suddenly couldn't drive any more. The
10 car kept going off onto the shoulder, y'know?

LINDA *(helpfully)*: Oh. Maybe it was the steering again. I don't think Angelo knows the Studebaker.

WILLY: No, it's me, it's me. Suddenly I realize I'm goin' sixty miles an hour and I don't remember the last five minutes. I'm – I
15 can't seem to – keep my mind to it.

LINDA: Maybe it's your glasses. You never went for your new glasses.

WILLY: No, I see everything. I came back ten miles an hour. It took me nearly four hours from Yonkers.

20 LINDA *(resigned)*: Well, you'll just have to take a rest, Willy, you can't continue this way.

WILLY: I just got back from Florida.

LINDA: But you didn't rest your mind. Your mind is overactive, and the mind is what counts, dear.

25 WILLY: I'll start out in the morning. Maybe I'll feel better in the morning. *(She is taking off his shoes.)* These goddam arch supports are killing me.

LINDA: Take an aspirin. Should I get you an aspirin? It'll soothe you.

30 WILLY *(with wonder)*: I was driving along, you understand? And I was fine. I was even observing the scenery. You can imagine, me looking at scenery, on the road every week of my life. But it's so beautiful up there, Linda, the trees are so thick, and the sun is warm. I opened the windshield and just let the warm
35 air bathe over me. And then all of a sudden I'm goin' off the road! I'm tellin' ya, I absolutely forgot I was driving. If I'd've

---

1 **to fade away** *here:* to become softer and softer until the sound can't be heard any more – 2 **numb** [nʌm] with no feeling – 2 **I couldn't make it.** I couldn't manage to drive to the place I wanted to go to. – 4 **delicately** [ˈ– – – –] so as not to upset – 6 **Yonkers** a city immediately north of New York City on the Hudson River – 10 **shoulder** *here:* the side of a road where a car with a breakdown can park – 12 **Studebaker** a make of car – 26 **arch support** sth put in a shoe for people with flat feet – 28 **to soothe** [suːð] to make sb feel calmer – 34 **windshield** *(A.E.)* windscreen *(B.E.)* (Until WWII many cars were manufactured with windshields that could be swung open.)

gone the other way over the white line I might've killed somebody. So I went on again – and five minutes later I'm dreamin'
again, and I nearly … *(He presses two fingers against his eyes.)*
I have such thoughts, I have such strange thoughts.

5 LINDA: Willy, dear. Talk to them again. There's no reason why
you can't work in New York.

WILLY: They don't need me in New York. I'm the New England
man. I'm vital in New England.

LINDA: But you're sixty years old. They can't expect you to keep
10 traveling every week.

WILLY: I'll have to send a wire to Portland. I'm supposed to see
Brown and Morrison tomorrow morning at ten o'clock to
show the line. Goddammit, I could sell them! *(He starts putting on his jacket.)*

15 LINDA *(taking the jacket from him)*: Why don't you go down to
the place tomorrow and tell Howard you've simply got to
work in New York? You're too accommodating, dear.

WILLY: If old man Wagner was alive I'd a been in charge of New
York now! That man was a prince, he was a masterful man.
20 But that boy of his, that Howard, he don't appreciate. When I
went north the first time, the Wagner Company didn't know
where New England was!

LINDA: Why don't you tell those things to Howard, dear?

WILLY *(encouraged)*: I will, I definitely will. Is there any cheese?
25 LINDA: I'll make you a sandwich.

WILLY: No, go to sleep. I'll take some milk. I'll be up right away.
The boys in?

LINDA: They're sleeping. Happy took Biff on a date tonight.

WILLY *(interested)*: That so?

30 LINDA: It was so nice to see them shaving together, one behind
the other, in the bathroom. And going out together. You
notice? The whole house smells of shaving lotion.

WILLY: Figure it out. Work a lifetime to pay off a house. You
finally own it, and there's nobody to live in it.

35 LINDA: Well, dear, life is a casting off. It's always that way.

---

1 **the white line** the line in the middle of a road – 8 **vital** ['vaɪtl] very important –
11 **wire** telegram – 11 **Portland** a city in the state of Maine – 13 **the line** the range
of products – 16 **the place** *here:* the main office – 17 **accommodating** [–'– – – –] very
or even too willing to help – 18 **I'd a been in charge of New York** I would have been
responsible for the New York City area – 19 **masterful** very competent – 20 **he don't
appreciate** *(coll.)* he doesn't appreciate my work – 28 **to take sb on a date** *here:* to take
sb to meet another person of the opposite sex – 32 **shaving lotion** perfume put on the
face after shaving – 33 **Figure it out.** Try to make sense of the whole thing. – 35 **to cast
off** to let go of things

WILLY: No, no, some people – some people accomplish something. Did Biff say anything after I went this morning?

LINDA: You shouldn't have criticized him, Willy, especially after he just got off the train. You mustn't lose your temper with
5   him.

WILLY: When the hell did I lose my temper? I simply asked him if he was making any money. Is that a criticism?

LINDA: But, dear, how could he make any money?

WILLY *(worried and angered)*: There's such an undercurrent in
10   him. He became a moody man. Did he apologize when I left this morning?

LINDA: He was crestfallen, Willy. You know how he admires you. I think if he finds himself, then you'll both be happier and not fight any more.

15   WILLY: How can he find himself on a farm? Is that a life? A farmhand? In the beginning, when he was young, I thought, well, a young man, it's good for him to tramp around, take a lot of different jobs. But it's more than ten years now and he has yet to make thirty-five dollars a week!

20   LINDA: He's finding himself, Willy.

WILLY: Not finding yourself at the age of thirty-four is a disgrace!

LINDA: Shh!

WILLY: The trouble is he's lazy, goddammit!

25   LINDA: Willy, please!

WILLY: Biff is a lazy bum!

LINDA: They're sleeping. Get something to eat. Go on down.

WILLY: Why did he come home? I would like to know what brought him home.

30   LINDA: I don't know. I think he's still lost, Willy. I think he's very lost.

WILLY: Biff Loman is lost. In the greatest country in the world a young man with such – personal attractiveness, gets lost. And such a hard worker. There's one thing about Biff – he's
35   not lazy.

LINDA: Never.

WILLY *(with pity and resolve)*: I'll see him in the morning; I'll have a nice talk with him. I'll get him a job selling. He could

---

4 **to lose one's temper** to suddenly become extremely angry – 9 **undercurrent** a hidden feeling – 12 **crestfallen** very disappointed, depressed – 15 **farmhand** farm worker – 21 **a disgrace** sth that brings shame – 26 **bum** person who avoids work, good-for-nothing – 27 **down** i. e. downstairs – 37 **with resolve** with determination

be big in no time. My God! Remember how they used to follow him around in high school? When he smiled at one of them their faces lit up. When he walked down the street ... *(He loses himself in reminiscences.)*

5 LINDA *(trying to bring him out of it)*: Willy, dear, I got a new kind of American-type cheese today. It's whipped.

WILLY: Why do you get American when I like Swiss?

LINDA: I just thought you'd like a change ...

WILLY: I don't want a change! I want Swiss cheese. Why am I
10 always being contradicted?

LINDA *(with a covering laugh)*: I thought it would be a surprise.

WILLY: Why don't you open a window in here, for God's sake?

LINDA *(with infinite patience)*: They're all open, dear.

WILLY: The way they boxed us in here. Bricks and windows, win-
15 dows and bricks.

LINDA: We should've bought the land next door.

WILLY: The street is lined with cars. There's not a breath of fresh air in the neighborhood. The grass don't grow any more, you can't raise a carrot in the back yard. They should've had a law
20 against apartment houses. Remember those two beautiful elm trees out there? When I and Biff hung the swing between them?

LINDA: Yeah, like being a million miles from the city.

WILLY: They should've arrested the builder for cutting those
25 down. They massacred the neighborhood. *(Lost.)* More and more I think of those days, Linda. This time of year it was lilac and wisteria. And then the peonies would come out, and the daffodils. What fragrance in this room!

LINDA: Well, after all, people had to move somewhere.

30 WILLY: No, there's more people now.

LINDA: I don't think there's more people. I think ...

WILLY: There's more people! That's what's ruining this country! Population is getting out of control. The competition is maddening! Smell the stink from that apartment house! And
35 another one on the other side ... How can they whip cheese?

---

1 **big** *here:* important – 3 **to light up** to become cheerful – 4 **reminiscences** [ˌremɪˈnɪsnsɪz] memories – 6 **to whip** to beat cream, eggs, etc – 10 **to contradict** [– –ˈ–] to express the opposite view – 11 **a covering laugh** *here:* a laugh to hide disappointment – 13 **infinite** [ˈɪnfɪnɪt] endless – 14 **brick** Ziegelstein – 19 **to raise** to grow – 21 **elm** Ulme – 21 **swing** a seat hanging by ropes or chains from a tree or frame – 25 **to massacre** *here:* to ruin – 26 **lilac** [ˈlaɪlək] Flieder – 27 **wisteria** [–ˈ– – –] a climbing plant with white flowers (Glyzine) – 27 **peony** [ˈpiːəni] Pfingstrose – 28 **daffodil** [ˈdɒfədɪl] Narzisse – 28 **fragrance** [ˈ– –] pleasant smell – 34 **maddening** enough to drive you crazy or make you very angry

(On Willy's last line, Biff and Happy raise themselves up in their beds, listening.)

LINDA: Go down, try it. And be quiet.

WILLY *(turning to Linda, guiltily)*: You're not worried about me,
5 are you, sweetheart?

BIFF: What's the matter?

HAPPY: Listen!

LINDA: You've got too much on the ball to worry about.

WILLY: You're my foundation and my support, Linda.

10 LINDA: Just try to relax, dear. You make mountains out of molehills.

WILLY: I won't fight with him any more. If he wants to go back
to Texas, let him go.

LINDA: He'll find his way.

15 WILLY: Sure. Certain men just don't get started till later in life.
Like Thomas Edison; I think. Or B. F. Goodrich. One of them
was deaf. *(He starts for the bedroom doorway.)* I'll put my
money on Biff.

LINDA: And Willy – if it's warm Sunday we'll drive in the country.
20 And we'll open the windshield, and take lunch.

WILLY: No, the windshields don't open on the new cars.

LINDA: But you opened it today.

WILLY: Me? I didn't. *(He stops.)* Now isn't that peculiar! Isn't that
a remarkable … *(He breaks off in amazement and fright as the*
25 *flute is heard distantly.)*

LINDA: What, darling?

WILLY: That is the most remarkable thing.

LINDA: What, dear?

WILLY: I was thinking of the Chevvy. *(Slight pause.)* Nineteen
30 twenty-eight … When I had that red Chevvy … *(Breaks off.)*
That funny? I coulda sworn I was driving that Chevvy today.

LINDA: Well, that's nothing. Something must've reminded you.

WILLY: Remarkable. Ts. Remember those days? The way Biff
used to simonize that car? The dealer refused to believe there

---

8 **You've got too much on the ball…** You are too competent … – 10 **You make mountains out of molehills.** You make unimportant things seem more important than they really are. – 10 **molehill** Maulwurfshügel – 16 **Thomas Edison** famous inventor (1841-1931) (He was partially deaf.) – 16 **B. F. Goodrich** American industrialist (1841-1888) – 17 **to put your money on sth or sb** to place a bet on sth or sb; *here:* to be sure that sb will be a success – 23 **peculiar** strange – 24 **to break off** *here:* to stop suddenly – 29 **Chevvy** ['ʃevi] Chevrolet, a low-priced car – 31 **coulda** *(coll.)* could have – 34 **to simonize** ['saɪmənaɪz] to polish a car with Simoniz (name of a wax sold in the U.S.A.)

was eighty thousand miles on it. *(He shakes his head.)* Heh! *(To Linda.)* Close your eyes, I'll be right up. *(He walks out of the bedroom.)*

HAPPY *(to Biff)*: Jesus, maybe he smashed up the car again!

5 LINDA *(calling after Willy)*: Be careful on the stairs, dear! The cheese is on the middle shelf *(She turns, goes over to the bed, takes his jacket, and goes out of the bedroom.)*

(Light has risen on the boys' room. Unseen, Willy is heard talking to himself, "eighty thousand miles," and a little laugh. Biff
10 *gets out of bed, comes downstage a bit, and stands attentively. Biff is two years older than his brother Happy, well built, but in these days bears a worn air and seems less self-assured. He has succeeded less, and his dreams are stronger and less acceptable than Happy's. Happy is tall, powerfully made. Sexuality is like*
15 *a visible color on him, or a scent that many women have discovered. He, like his brother, is lost, but in a different way, for he has never allowed himself to turn his face toward defeat and is thus more confused and hard-skinned, although seemingly more content.)*

20 HAPPY *(getting out of bed)*: He's going to get his license taken away if he keeps that up. I'm getting nervous about him, y'know, Biff?

BIFF: His eyes are going.

HAPPY: I've driven with him. He sees all right. He just doesn't
25 keep his mind on it. I drove into the city with him last week. He stops at a green light and then it turns red and he goes. *(He laughs.)*

BIFF: Maybe he's color-blind.

HAPPY: Pop? Why he's got the finest eye for color in the business.
30 You know that.

BIFF *(sitting down on his bed)*: I'm going to sleep.

HAPPY: You're not still sour on Dad, are you, Biff?

BIFF: He's all right, I guess.

WILLY *(underneath them, in the living room)*: Yes, sir, eighty
35 thousand miles - eighty-two thousand!

BIFF: You smoking?

---

4 **to smash up** *here:* to have a serious accident – 12 **to bear a worn air** to have a tired appearance and expression – 12 **self-assured** self-confident – 14 **powerfully made** with a very strong body – 15 **scent** [sent] pleasant smell – 18 **hard-skinned** not easily upset by criticism, not sensitive – 20 **license** driver's license – 23 **his eyes are going** his eyes are getting steadily worse – 29 **Pop** Dad, Father – 32 **to be sour on sb** to be angry with sb

HAPPY *(holding out a pack of cigarettes)*: Want one?

BIFF: *(taking a cigarette)*: I can never sleep when I smell it.

WILLY: What a simonizing job, heh?

HAPPY *(with deep sentiment)*: Funny, Biff, y'know? Us sleeping
5   in here again? The old beds. *(He pats his bed affectionately.)*
    All the talk that went across those two beds, huh? Our whole
    lives.

BIFF: Yeah. Lotta dreams and plans.

HAPPY *(with a deep and masculine laugh)*: About five hundred
10   women would like to know what was said in this room. *(They
    share a soft laugh.)*

BIFF: Remember that big Betsy something – what the hell was
    her name over on Bushwick Avenue?

HAPPY *(combing his hair)*: With the collie dog!

15 BIFF: That's the one. I got you in there, remember?

HAPPY: Yeah, that was my first time – I think. Boy, there was a
    pig. *(They laugh, almost crudely.)* You taught me everything I
    know about women. Don't forget that.

BIFF: I bet you forgot how bashful you used to be. Especially
20   with girls.

HAPPY: Oh, I still am, Biff.

BIFF: Oh, go on.

HAPPY: I just control it, that's all. I think I got less bashful and you
    got more so. What happened, Biff? Where's the old humor, the
25   old confidence? *(He shakes Biff's knee. Biff gets up and moves
    restlessly about the room.)* What's the matter?

BIFF: Why does Dad mock me all the time?

HAPPY: He's not mocking you, he …

BIFF: Everything I say there's a twist of mockery on his face. I
30   can't get near him.

HAPPY: He just wants you to make good, that's all. I wanted to
    talk to you about Dad for a long time, Biff. Something's – hap-
    pening to him. He – talks to himself.

BIFF: I noticed that this morning. But he always mumbled.

35 HAPPY: But not so noticeable. It got so embarrassing I sent him
    to Florida. And you know something? Most of the time he's
    talking to you.

---

5 **to pat** to tap gently – 8 **a lotta** *(coll.)* a lot of – 15 **I got you in there.** I made it possible for you to have sex with her. – 17 **pig** *here:* a fat and ugly female – 17 **crudely**
vulgarly – 19 **bashful** shy or timid – 22 **Oh, go on.** I don't believe you. – 27 **to mock sb** to
make fun of sb – 29 **a twist of mockery on his face** an expression on his face as if he
was making fun of me – 29 **I can't get near him.** I can't establish a close relationship
with him. – 31 **to make good** to be successful – 34 **to mumble** to speak quietly and
without opening one's mouth properly

BIFF: What's he say about me?

HAPPY: I can't make it out.

BIFF: What's he say about me?

HAPPY: I think the fact that you're not settled, that you're still
5   kind of up in the air …

BIFF: There's one or two other things depressing him, Happy.

HAPPY: What do you mean?

BIFF: Never mind. Just don't lay it all to me.

HAPPY: But I think if you just got started – I mean – is there any
10   future for you out there?

BIFF: I tell ya, Hap, I don't know what the future is. I don't know
    – what I'm supposed to want.

HAPPY: What do you mean?

BIFF: Well, I spent six or seven years after high school trying to
15   work myself up. Shipping clerk, salesman, business of one
    kind or another. And it's a measly manner of existence. To get
    on that subway on the hot mornings in summer. To devote
    your whole life to keeping stock, or making phone calls, or
    selling or buying. To suffer fifty weeks of the year for the sake
20   of a two-week vacation, when all you really desire is to be out-
    doors, with your shirt off. And always to have to get ahead of
    the next fella. And still – that's how you build a future.

HAPPY: Well, you really enjoy it on a farm? Are you content out
    there?

25 BIFF *(with rising agitation)*: Hap, I've had twenty or thirty dif-
    ferent kinds of jobs since I left home before the war, and it
    always turns out the same. I just realized it lately. In Nebraska
    when I herded cattle, and the Dakotas, and Arizona, and now
    in Texas. It's why I came home now, I guess, because I realized
30   it. This farm I work on, it's spring there now, see? And they've
    got about fifteen new colts. There's nothing more inspiring or
    – beautiful than the sight of a mare and a new colt. And it's
    cool there now, see? Texas is cool now, and it's spring. And
    whenever spring comes to where I am, I suddenly get the
35   feeling, my God, I'm not gettin' anywhere! What the hell am
    I doing, playing around with horses, twenty-eight dollars a

---

2 **to make sth out** to understand sth – 4 **to be settled** to have a job and somewhere
permanent to live – 5 **up in the air** without any set goal – 8 **Just don't lay it all to me.**
Don't blame me for everything. – 15 **shipping clerk** a person who manages the ship-
ment of goods – 16 **measly** *(sl.)* miserable – 17 **to devote one's life to** to spend one's
life doing sth – 18 **to keep stock** to make sure that there are always enough goods
available in the warehouse – 22 **fella** *(coll.)* fellow – 23 **content** [–'–] happy, satisfied –
25 **agitation** emotion, anger – 28 **to herd cattle** to take care of cattle – 31 **colt** [kɒlt] a
young male horse – 32 **mare** a female horse

week! I'm thirty-four years old, I oughta be makin' my future. That's when I come running home. And now, I get here, and I don't know what to do with myself. *(After a pause.)* I've always made a point of not wasting my life, and everytime I come
5   back here I know that all I've done is to waste my life.

HAPPY: You're a poet, you know that, Biff? You're a – you're an idealist!

BIFF: No, I'm mixed up very bad. Maybe I oughta get married. Maybe I oughta get stuck into something. Maybe that's my
10   trouble. I'm like a boy. I'm not married, I'm not in business, I just – I'm like a boy. Are you content, Hap? You're a success, aren't you? Are you content?

HAPPY: Hell, no!

BIFF: Why? You're making money, aren't you?

15 HAPPY *(moving about with energy, expressiveness)*: All I can do now is wait for the merchandise manager to die. And suppose I get to be merchandise manager? He's a good friend of mine, and he just built a terrific estate on Long Island. And he lived there about two months and sold it, and now he's
20   building another one. He can't enjoy it once it's finished. And I know that's just what I would do. I don't know what the hell I'm workin' for. Sometimes I sit in my apartment – all alone. And I think of the rent I'm paying. And it's crazy. But then, it's what I always wanted. My own apartment, a car, and plenty of
25   women. And still, goddammit, I'm lonely.

BIFF *(with enthusiasm)*: Listen, why don't you come out West with me?

HAPPY: You and I, heh?

BIFF: Sure, maybe we could buy a ranch. Raise cattle, use our
30   muscles. Men built like we are should be working out in the open.

HAPPY *(avidly)*: The Loman Brothers, heh?

BIFF *(with vast affection)*: Sure, we'd be known all over the counties!

35 HAPPY *(enthralled)*: That's what I dream about, Biff. Sometimes I want to just rip my clothes off in the middle of the store and outbox that goddam merchandise manager. I mean I can out-

---

1 **oughta** *(coll.)* ought to – 9 **to get stuck into sth** *(coll.)* to get really involved in sth – 15 **with expressiveness** showing one's feelings and emotions – 16 **merchandise manager** ['– – –] the person responsible for the selling and buying of goods – 18 **terrific estate** [ɪ'steɪt] an impressive house with a lot of land around it – 23 **rent** money you pay for the use of an apartment or house – 32 **avidly** ['ævɪdli] enthusiastically – 33 **vast** a lot of – 33 **affection** fondness – 35 **enthralled** [ɪn'θrɔːld] captivated, paying complete attention – 37 **to outbox sb** [–'–] to defeat sb in a boxing match

box, outrun, and outlift anybody in that store, and I have to
take orders from those common, petty sons-of-bitches till I
can't stand it any more.

BIFF: I'm tellin' you, kid, if you were with me I'd be happy out
there.

HAPPY *(enthused)*: See, Biff, everybody around me is so false
that I'm constantly lowering my ideals ...

BIFF: Baby, together we'd stand up for one another, we'd have
someone to trust.

HAPPY: If I were around you ...

BIFF: Hap, the trouble is we weren't brought up to grub for
money. I don't know how to do it.

HAPPY: Neither can I!

BIFF: Then let's go!

HAPPY: The only thing is – what can you make out there?

BIFF: But look at your friend. Builds an estate and then hasn't
the peace of mind to live in it.

HAPPY: Yeah, but when he walks into the store the waves part in
front of him. That's fifty-two thousand dollars a year coming
through the revolving door, and I got more in my pinky finger
than he's got in his head.

BIFF: Yeah, but you just said ...

HAPPY: I gotta show some of those pompous, self-important
executives over there that Hap Loman can make the grade.
I want to walk into the store the way he walks in. Then I'll go
with you, Biff. We'll be together yet, I swear. But take those
two we had tonight. Now weren't they gorgeous creatures?

BIFF: Yeah, yeah, most gorgeous I've had in years.

HAPPY: I get that any time I want, Biff. Whenever I feel disgusted.
The only trouble is, it gets like bowling or something. I just
keep knockin' them over and it doesn't mean anything. You
still run around a lot?

---

1 **to outrun sb** [–'–] to run faster than sb else – 1 **to outlift sb** [–'–] to lift heavier
weights than sb else – 2 **petty** unimportant and small-minded – 2 **son-of-a-bitch** *(sl.)*
sb one thoroughly dislikes – 6 **enthused** *(coll.)* enthusiastic – 8 **baby** *(sl.)* a young man
or woman that one is fond of – 8 **to stand up for sb** to defend sb, to side with sb –
11 **to grub** *here:* to work hard – 20 **revolving door** an entrance consisting of four doors
which turn together in a circle when pushed – 20 **pinky finger** the smallest finger on
the hand – 23 **gotta** *(coll.)* have to – 23 **pompous** showing too much self-importance –
24 **executive** [ɪgˈzekjətɪv] a person who manages a business – 24 **to make the grade** to
succeed – 26 **yet** in spite of everything – 27 **gorgeous** [ˈgɔːdʒəs] attractive – 29 **to feel
disgusted** to feel sickened about sth – 31 **to knock sb over** *here:* to be very attractive
to others and very successful with them – 32 **to run around a lot** *here:* to go out with a
lot of women

BIFF: Naa. I'd like to find a girl – steady, somebody with sub-
stance.

HAPPY: That's what I long for.

BIFF: Go on! You'd never come home.

5 HAPPY: I would! Somebody with character, with resistance! Like
Mom, y'know? You're gonna call me a bastard when I tell you
this. That girl Charlotte I was with tonight is engaged to be
married in five weeks. *(He tries on his new hat.)*

BIFF: No kiddin'!

10 HAPPY: Sure, the guy's in line for the vice-presidency of the store.
I don't know what gets into me, maybe I just have an overde-
veloped sense of competition or something, but I went and
ruined her, and furthermore I can't get rid of her. And he's the
third executive I've done that to. Isn't that a crummy charac-

15 teristic? And to top it all, I go to their weddings! *(Indignantly,
but laughing.)* Like I'm not supposed to take bribes. Manufac-
turers offer me a hundred-dollar bill now and then to throw
an order their way. You know how honest I am, but it's like this
girl, see. I hate myself for it. Because I don't want the girl, and

20 still, I take it and – I love it!

BIFF: Let's go to sleep.

HAPPY: I guess we didn't settle anything, heh?

BIFF: I just got one idea that I think I'm going to try.

HAPPY: What's that?

25 BIFF: Remember Bill Oliver?

HAPPY: Sure, Oliver is very big now. You want to work for him
again?

BIFF: No, but when I quit he said something to me. He put his
arm on my shoulder, and he said, "Biff, if you ever need any-

30 thing, come to me."

HAPPY: I remember that. That sounds good.

BIFF: I think I'll go to see him. If I could get ten thousand or
even seven or eight thousand dollars I could buy a beautiful
ranch.

---

1 **a steady girl** a girl who is one's only girlfriend for a long time – 6 **gonna** *(coll.)* going
to – 7 **to be engaged to be married** to have agreed to marry sb in the near future –
9 **No kiddin'!** *(coll.)* Is that really true? – 10 **to be in line for sth** to be the next to get
sth – 13 **to ruin sb** *here:* to have sex with a woman for whom it is the first time, and so
ruin her reputation – 14 **crummy** *(sl.)* miserable – 15 **to top it all** in addition to this –
15 **indignantly** [–'– – –] angrily because one feels one has been treated unjustly –
16 **to take bribes** to accept money from sb in return for doing sth (usually dishonest)
for them – 17 **to throw an order their way** to order products from them – 28 **to quit**
here: to leave a job

HAPPY: I bet he'd back you. Cause he thought highly of you, Biff. I mean, they all do. You're well liked, Biff. That's why I say to come back here, and we both have the apartment. And I'm tellin' you, Biff, any babe you want …

5 BIFF: No, with a ranch I could do the work I like and still be something. I just wonder though. I wonder if Oliver still thinks I stole that carton of basketballs.

HAPPY: Oh, he probably forgot that long ago. It's almost ten years. You're too sensitive. Anyway, he didn't really fire you.

10 BIFF: Well, I think he was going to. I think that's why I quit. I was never sure whether he knew or not. I know he thought the world of me, though. I was the only one he'd let lock up the place.

WILLY *(below)*: You gonna wash the engine, Biff?

15 HAPPY: Shh!

(Biff looks at Happy, who is gazing down, listening. Willy is mumbling in the parlor.)

HAPPY: You hear that?

(They listen. Willy laughs warmly.)

20 BIFF *(growing angry)*: Doesn't he know Mom can hear that?
WILLY: Don't get your sweater dirty, Biff!

(A look of pain crosses Biff's face.)

HAPPY: Isn't that terrible? Don't leave again, will you? You'll find a job here. You gotta stick around. I don't know what to do
25 about him, it's getting embarrassing.
WILLY: What a simonizing job!
BIFF: Mom's hearing that!
WILLY: No kiddin', Biff, you got a date? Wonderful!
HAPPY: Go on to sleep. But talk to him in the morning, will you?
30 BIFF *(reluctantly getting into bed)*: With her in the house. Brother!
HAPPY *(getting into bed)*: I wish you'd have a good talk with him.

(The light on their room begins to fade.)

35 BIFF *(to himself in bed)*: That selfish, stupid …

1 **to back sb** *here:* to support sb with money – 4 **babe** *(sl.)* young woman – 11 **to think the world of sb** to have a very good opinion of sb – 16 **to gaze** to look with fixed attention – 24 **to stick around** to stay for a while – 30 **reluctantly** unwillingly – 31 **Brother!** What a terrible thought!

HAPPY: Sh … Sleep, Biff.

(Their light is out. Well before they have finished speaking, Willy's form is dimly seen below in the darkened kitchen. He opens the refrigerator, searches in there, and takes out a bottle
5 *of milk. The apartment houses are fading out, and the entire house and surroundings become covered with leaves. Music insinuates itself as the leaves appear.)*

WILLY: Just wanna be careful with those girls, Biff, that's all. Don't make any promises. No promises of any kind. Because a girl,
10 y'know, they always believe what you tell 'em, and you're very young, Biff, you're too young to be talking seriously to girls.

(Light rises on the kitchen. Willy, talking, shuts the refrigerator door and comes downstage to the kitchen table. He pours milk into a glass. He is totally immersed in himself, smiling faintly.)

15 WILLY: Too young entirely, Biff. You want to watch your schooling first. Then when you're all set, there'll be plenty of girls
for a boy like you. *(He smiles broadly at a kitchen chair.)* That
so? The girls pay for you? *(He laughs)* Boy, you must really be
makin' a hit.

20 *(Willy is gradually addressing – physically – a point offstage, speaking through the wall of the kitchen, and his voice has been rising in volume to that of a normal conversation.)*

WILLY: I been wondering why you polish the car so careful. Ha!
Don't leave the hubcaps, boys. Get the chamois to the hub-
25 caps. Happy, use newspaper on the windows, it's the easiest
thing. Show him how to do it Biff! You see, Happy? Pad it up,
use it like a pad. That's it, that's it, good work. You're doin' all
right, Hap. *(He pauses, then nods in approbation for a few sec-
onds, then looks upward.)* Biff, first thing we gotta do when
30 we get time is clip that big branch over the house. Afraid it's

---

2 **well before** a long time before – 7 **to insinuate** *here:* to slowly become loud enough
to hear – 8 **wanna** *(sl.)* want to;*here:* you should – 14 **to be immersed in oneself** to be
so completely involved in oneself that one is unaware of anything else that is going
on – 14 **faintly** just a little bit – 15 **schooling** education – 16 **set** finished, ready – 18 **boy**
an expression used to show excitement – 19 **to make a hit** to be a great success –
20 **offstage** see glossary – 22 **to rise in volume** to become louder – 24 **hubcap** metal
covering on the middle of a wheel – 24 **get the chamois to the hubcaps** wipe the
hubcaps with the chamois – 24 **chamois** ['ʃɪmi] a piece of soft leather used for wiping
and polishing – 26 **pad it up** *here:* fold it up so that it is like a pad – 27 **pad** thick, flat
cloth – 28 **approbation** [ˌ– –ˈ– –] approval – 30 **to clip** to cut back

gonna fall in a storm and hit the roof. Tell you what. We get a rope and sling her around, and then we climb up there with a couple of saws and take her down. Soon as you finish the car, boys, I wanna see ya. I got a surprise for you, boys.

5 BIFF *(offstage)*: Whatta ya got, Dad?

WILLY: No, you finish first. Never leave a job till you're finished – remember that. *(Looking toward the "big trees.")* Biff, up in Albany I saw a beautiful hammock. I think I'll buy it next trip, and we'll hang it right between those two elms. Wouldn't that
10 be something? Just swingin' there under those branches. Boy, that would be …

(Young Biff and Young Happy appear from the direction Willy was addressing. Happy carries rags and a pail of water. Biff, wearing a sweater with a block "S," carries a football.)

15 BIFF *(pointing in the direction of the car offstage)*: How's that, Pop, professional?

WILLY: Terrific. Terrific job, boys. Good work, Biff …

HAPPY: Where's the surprise, Pop?

WILLY: In the back seat of the car.

20 HAPPY: Boy! *(He runs off.)*

BIFF: What is it, Dad? Tell me, what'd you buy?

WILLY *(laughing, cuffs him)*: Never mind, something I want you to have.

BIFF *(turns and starts off)*: What is it, Hap?

25 HAPPY *(offstage)*: It's a punching bag!

BIFF: Oh, Pop!

WILLY: It's got Gene Tunney's signature on it!

(Happy runs onstage with a punching bag.)

BIFF: Gee, how'd you know we wanted a punching bag?

30 WILLY: Well, it's the finest thing for the timing.

HAPPY *(lies down on his back and pedals with his feet)*: I'm losing weight, you notice, Pop?

WILLY *(to Happy)*: Jumping rope is good too.

---

5 **whatta ya got** *(coll.)* what have you got – 8 **hammock** ['hɒmək] a piece of cloth hung between two posts and used as a bed – 13 **pail** bucket – 14 **a block "S"** a big "S" – 16 **professional** *here:* a first rate job – 22 **to cuff sb** to hit sb with the hand in a light friendly way – 27 **Gene Tunney** famous American heavyweight boxer (1898-1978) – 28 **punching bag** heavy bag hanging on a rope used by boxers for training – 29 **gee** [dʒiː] expression of surprise and wonder – 31 **to pedal** ['pedl] to move one's feet and legs as if riding a bicycle – 33 **to jump rope** to jump over a rope which is being swung round the head and feet

BIFF: Did you see the new football I got?

WILLY *(examining the ball)*: Where'd you get a new ball?

BIFF: The coach told me to practice my passing.

WILLY: That so? And he gave you the ball, heh?

5 BIFF: Well, I borrowed it from the locker room. *(He laughs confidentially.)*

WILLY *(laughing with him at the theft)*: I want you to return that.

HAPPY: I told you he wouldn't like it!

10 BIFF *(angrily)*: Well, I'm bringing it back!

WILLY *(stopping the incipient argument, to Happy)*: Sure, he's gotta practice with a regulation ball, doesn't he? *(To Biff.)* Coach'll probably congratulate you on your initiative!

BIFF: Oh, he keeps congratulating my initiative all the time,
15 Pop.

WILLY: That's because he likes you. If somebody else took that ball there'd be an uproar. So what's the report, boys, what's the report?

BIFF: Where'd you go this time, Dad? Gee we were lonesome for
20 you.

WILLY *(pleased, puts an arm around each boy and they come down to the apron)*: Lonesome, heh?

BIFF: Missed you every minute.

WILLY: Don't say? Tell you a secret, boys. Don't breathe it to a
25 soul. Someday I'll have my own business, and I'll never have to leave home any more.

HAPPY: Like Uncle Charley, heh?

WILLY: Bigger than Uncle Charley! Because Charley is not – liked. He's liked, but he's not – well liked.

30 BIFF: Where'd you go this time, Dad?

WILLY: Well, I got on the road, and I went north to Providence. Met the Mayor.

BIFF: The Mayor of Providence!

WILLY: He was sitting in the hotel lobby.

35 BIFF: What'd he say?

WILLY: He said, "Morning!" And I said, "You got a fine city here, Mayor." And then he had coffee with me. And then I went to

---

3 **coach** a person who trains a team – 3 **to pass** to throw or kick a ball to another person in the team – 4 **heh?** [eɪ] did he? – 5 **locker room** room where you change Your clothes at a sports field – 5 **confidentially** [– –ˈ– – –] as if telling a secret – 11 **incipient** [ɪnˈsɪpiənt] just beginning – 12 **regulation ball** a ball of the official size, as used in official games – 17 **uproar** [ˈʌprɔː] noise and shouting made by people who are angry – 18 **report** *here:* situation, state of things – 24 **Don't breathe it to a soul.** Don't tell anyone about it. – 31 **Providence** the capital of the state of Rhode Island

Waterbury. Waterbury is a fine city. Big clock city, the famous Waterbury clock. Sold a nice bill there. And then Boston – Boston is the cradle of the Revolution. A fine city. And a couple of other towns in Mass., and on to Portland and Bangor and
5   straight home!

BIFF: Gee, I'd love to go with you sometime, Dad.

WILLY: Soon as summer comes.

HAPPY: Promise?

WILLY: You and Hap and I, and I'll show you all the towns. Amer-
10   ica is full of beautiful towns and fine, upstanding people. And they know me, boys, they know me up and down New England. The finest people. And when I bring you fellas up, there'll be open sesame for all of us, 'cause one thing, boys: I have friends. I can park my car in any street in New England,
15   and the cops protect it like their own. This summer, heh?

BIFF AND HAPPY *(together)*: Yeah! You bet!

WILLY: We'll take our bathing suits.

HAPPY: We'll carry your bags, Pop!

WILLY: Oh, won't that be something! Me comin' into the Boston
20   stores with you boys carryin' my bags. What a sensation!

(Biff is prancing around, practicing passing the ball.)

WILLY: You nervous, Biff, about the game?

BIFF: Not if you're gonna be there.

WILLY: What do they say about you in school, now that they
25   made you captain?

HAPPY: There's a crowd of girls behind him everytime the classes change.

BIFF *(taking Willy's hand)*: This Saturday, Pop, this Saturday – just for you, I'm going to break through for a touchdown.

30   HAPPY: You're supposed to pass.

---

1 **Waterbury** ['– – –] city in the state of Connecticut – 1 **big clock city** city known for manufacturing clocks – 2 **to sell a nice bill** to make a lot of sales – 3 **cradle** *here:* the place where sth began – 4 **Mass.** short for Massachusetts – 4 **Bangor** ['bɔŋgər] a city in Maine – 10 **upstanding** honest – 13 **open sesame** ['sesəmi] open doors, we'll be welcome – 15 **cop** *(sl.)* policeman – 16 **You bet!** We definitely will! – 21 **to prance** [ ] to jump around gaily – 25 **captain** leader of a team – 26 **everytime the classes change** during the breaks between lessons when students go to another classroom – 29 **to break through** to get through the other team's defensive line – 29 **touchdown** in American football: when a player takes the ball over the goal line and so scores points for his team.

BIFF: I'm takin' one play for Pop. You watch me, Pop, and when I take off my helmet, that means I'm breakin' out. Then you watch me crash through that line!

WILLY *(kisses Biff)*: Oh, wait'll I tell this in Boston!

5 *(Bernard enters in knickers. He is younger than Biff, earnest and loyal, a worried boy).*

BERNARD: Biff, where are you? You're supposed to study with me today.

WILLY: Hey, looka Bernard. What're you lookin' so anemic about, 10 Bernard?

BERNARD: He's gotta study, Uncle Willy. He's got Regents next week.

HAPPY *(tauntingly, spinning Bernard around)*: Let's box, Bernard!

15 BERNARD: Biff! *(He gets away from Happy.)* Listen, Biff, I heard Mr. Birnbaum say that if you don't start studyin' math he's gonna flunk you, and you won't graduate. I heard him!

WILLY: You better study with him, Biff. Go ahead now.

BERNARD: I heard him!

20 BIFF: Oh, Pop, you didn't see my sneakers! *(He holds up a foot for Willy to look at.)*

WILLY: Hey, that's a beautiful job of printing!

BERNARD *(wiping his glasses)*: Just because he printed University of Virginia on his sneakers doesn't mean they've got to gradu-25 ate him. Uncle Willy!

WILLY *(angrily)*: What're you talking about? With scholarships to three universities they're gonna flunk him?

BERNARD: But I heard Mr. Birnbaum say …

WILLY: Don't be a pest, Bernard! *(To his boys.)* What an anemic!

30 BERNARD: Okay, I'm waiting for you in my house, Biff. *(Bernard goes off. The Lomans laugh.)*

WILLY: Bernard is not well liked, is he?

---

1 **I'm takin' one play for Pop.** One time I'm going to make a touchdown especially for father. – 2 **to break out** *here:* to break through – 3 **line** the line of defensive players on the other team – 5 **knickers** ['nɪkəz] (AE) knickerbockers, trousers that reach as far as the knees – 9 **looka** *(coll.)* look at – 9 **anemic** [ə'niːmɪk] pale and tired, unhealthy – 11 **Regents** ['riːdʒənts] a test that all students in the state of New York must pass in order to get their high school diploma – 13 **tauntingly** ['tɔːntɪŋli] in such a way as to upset and annoy – 13 **to spin sb around** to cause sb to turn around – 17 **to flunk sb** to give sb poor marks so that they fail – 17 **to graduate** to finish high school or a university education with a diploma or degree – 20 **sneakers** ['sniːkəz] light sports shoes – 26 **scholarship** ['skɒləʃɪp] financial aid given to a student with particular academic or sporting ability – 29 **pest** an annoying person

BIFF: He's liked, but he's not well liked.

HAPPY: That's right, Pop.

WILLY: That's just what I mean. Bernard can get the best marks in school, y'understand, but when he gets out in the business
5 world, y'understand, you are going to be five times ahead of him. That's why I thank Almighty God you're both built like Adonises. Because the man who makes an appearance in the business world, the man who creates personal interest, is the man who gets ahead. Be liked and you will never want.
10 You take me, for instance. I never have to wait in line to see a buyer. "Willy Loman is here!" That's all they have to know, and I go right through.

BIFF: Did you knock them dead, Pop?

WILLY: Knocked 'em cold in Providence, slaughtered 'em in
15 Boston.

HAPPY *(on his back, pedaling again)*: I'm losing weight, you notice, Pop?

(Linda enters as of old, a ribbon in her hair, carrying a basket of washing.)

20 LINDA *(with youthful energy)*: Hello, dear!

WILLY: Sweetheart!

LINDA: How'd the Chevvy run?

WILLY: Chevrolet, Linda, is the greatest car ever built. *(To the boys.)* Since when do you let your mother carry wash up the
25 stairs?

BIFF: Grab hold there, boy!

HAPPY: Where to, Mom?

LINDA: Hang them up on the line. And you better go down to your friends, Biff. The cellar is full of boys. They don't know
30 what to do with themselves.

BIFF: Ah, when Pop comes home they can wait!

WILLY *(laughs appreciatively)*: You better go down and tell them what to do, Biff.

BIFF: I think I'll have them sweep out the furnace room.

35 WILLY: Good work, Biff.

---

7 **Adonis** [ə'dɒnɪs] young man in Greek mythology who was loved by a goddess because of his beauty, *here:* a young man of physical beauty – 9 **to get ahead** to be successful – 9 **to want** to be needy – 14 **to knock sb dead, to knock sb cold, to slaughter sb** *here:* to be very successful as a businessman, doing better than all the other competitors – 18 **as of old** as in the past – 26 **to grab hold** to suddenly seize sth – 32 **appreciatively** [ə'priːʃətɪvli] showing admiration – 34 **furnace room** ['fɜːnɪs] cellar room in which coal, oil, etc. is stored and is turned into heat for the central heating system

BIFF *(goes through wall-line of kitchen to doorway at back and calls down)*: Fellas! Everybody sweep out the furnace room! I'll be right down!

VOICES: All right! Okay, Biff.

5 BIFF: George and Sam and Frank, come out back! We're hangin' up the wash! Come on, Hap, on the double! *(He and Happy carry out the basket.)*

LINDA: The way they obey him!

WILLY: Well, that's training, the training. I'm tellin' you, I was
10 sellin' thousands and thousands, but I had to come home.

LINDA: Oh, the whole block'll be at that game. Did you sell anything?

WILLY: I did five hundred gross in Providence and seven hundred gross in Boston.

15 LINDA: No! Wait a minute, I've got a pencil. *(She pulls pencil and paper out of her apron pocket.)* That makes your commission Two hundred – my God! Two hundred and twelve dollars!

WILLY: Well, I didn't figure it yet, but …

LINDA: How much did you do?

20 WILLY: Well, I – I did – about a hundred and eighty gross in Providence. Well, no – it came to – roughly two hundred gross on the whole trip.

LINDA *(without hesitation)*: Two hundred gross. That's … *(She figures.)*

25 WILLY: The trouble was that three of the stores were half-closed for inventory in Boston. Otherwise I woulda broke records.

LINDA: Well, it makes seventy dollars and some pennies. That's very good.

WILLY: What do we owe?

30 LINDA: Well, on the first there's sixteen dollars on the refrigerator …

WILLY: Why sixteen?

LINDA: Well, the fan belt broke, so it was a dollar eighty.

WILLY: But it's brand new.

35 LINDA: Well, the man said that's the way it is. Till they work themselves in, y'know.

---

2 **fellas** *(coll.)* fellows – 6 **on the double** (military expression) quickly – 11 **the whole block** all the neighbors – 13 **I did five hundred gross.** [ɡrəʊs] I sold \$500 worth of goods. – 16 **commission** [‑ˈ‑ ‑] a percentage of the money from sales that a salesman can keep for himself – 21 **it came to** the total amount was – 21 **roughly** [ˈrʌfli] approximately – 26 **inventory** the listing of all the goods and material in stock – 26 **I woulda broke records.** I would have done better than ever before – 33 **fan belt** Ventilatorriemen – 35 **Till they work themselves in** Until all the moving parts of the new apparatus work properly together

(They move through the wall-line into the kitchen.)

WILLY: I hope we didn't get stuck on that machine.

LINDA: They got the biggest ads of any of them!

WILLY: I know, it's a fine machine. What else?

5 LINDA: Well, there's nine-sixty for the washing machine. And for the vacuum cleaner there's three and a half due on the fifteenth. Then the roof, you got twenty-one dollars remaining.

WILLY: It don't leak, does it?

LINDA: No, they did a wonderful job. Then you owe Frank for the
10 carburetor.

WILLY: I'm not going to pay that man! That goddam Chevrolet, they ought to prohibit the manufacture of that car!

LINDA: Well, you owe him three and a half. And odds and ends, comes to around a hundred and twenty dollars by the fif-
15 teenth.

WILLY: A hundred and twenty dollars! My God, if business don't pick up I don't know what I'm gonna do!

LINDA: Well, next week you'll do better.

WILLY: Oh, I'll knock 'em dead next week. I'll go to Hartford. I'm
20 very well liked in Hartford. You know, the trouble is, Linda, people don't seem to take to me.

(They move onto the forestage.)

LINDA: Oh, don't be foolish.

WILLY: I know it when I walk in. They seem to laugh at me.

25 LINDA: Why? Why would they laugh at you? Don't talk that way, Willy.

(Willy moves to the edge of the stage. Linda goes into the kitchen and starts to darn stockings.)

WILLY: I don't know the reason for it, but they just pass me by.
30 I'm not noticed.

LINDA: But you're doing wonderful, dear. You're making seventy to a hundred dollars a week.

---

2 **to get stuck on sth** to buy sth that later turns out to be poor quality – 3 **ad** short form for advertisement – 6 **vacuum cleaner** machine for cleaning dust etc. from carpets and floors – 6 **due** that should be paid – 9 **to owe sb sth** to have to pay sb sth – 10 **carburetor** [ˌkɑːbjʊˈretə] apparatus in a car that supplies the engine wih a mixture of fuel and air (Vergaser) – 13 **odds and ends** a few small items – 17 **to pick up** to improve – 19 **Hartford** capital of Connecticut – 21 **to take to sb** to become fond of sb – 28 **to darn** to mend a hole in a sock, shirt, etc.

WILLY: But I gotta be at it ten, twelve hours a day. Other men – I
don't know – they do it easier. I don't know why – I can't stop
myself – I talk too much. A man oughta come in with a few
words. One thing about Charley. He's a man of few words, and
5   they respect him.
LINDA: You don't talk too much, you're just lively.
WILLY *(smiling)*: Well, I figure, what the hell, life is short, a couple of jokes. *(To himself.)* I joke too much. *(The smile goes.)*
LINDA: Why? You're …
10   WILLY: I'm fat. I'm very – foolish to look at, Linda. I didn't tell
you, but Christmas time I happened to be calling on F. H.
Stewarts, and a salesman I know, as I was going in to see the
buyer I heard him say something about – walrus. And I – I
cracked him right across the face. I won't take that. I simply
15   will not take that. But they do laugh at me. I know that.
LINDA: Darling …
WILLY: I gotta overcome it. I know I gotta overcome it. I'm not
dressing to advantage, maybe.
LINDA: Willy, darling, you're the handsomest man in the
20   world …
WILLY: Oh, no, Linda.
LINDA: To me you are. *(Slight pause.)* The handsomest.

*(From the darkness is heard the laughter of a woman. Willy
doesn't turn to it, but it continues through Linda's lines.)*

25   LINDA: And the boys, Willy. Few men are idolized by their children the way you are.

*(Music is heard as behind a scrim, to the left of the house; The
Woman, dimly seen, is dressing.)*

WILLY *(with great feeling)*: You're the best there is, Linda, you're
30   a pal, you know that? On the road – on the road I want to grab
you sometimes and just kiss the life outa you.

*(The laughter is loud now, and he moves into a brightening
area at the left, where The Woman has come from behind the
scrim and is standing, putting on her hat, looking into a "mir-
35   ror" and laughing.)*

---

1 **I gotta be at it** I have to be doing it – 11 **to call on sb** to make a short visit – 13 **walrus**
['wɒlrəs] Walross – 14 **to crack sb** to strike sb – 14 **I won't take that.** I won't tolerate
that. – 18 **to dress to advantage** to wear clothes that make a good impression on other
people – 25 **to idolize sb** ['aɪ– –] to admire sb very much – 27 **scrim** thin curtain that
can be seen through – 30 **pal** *(coll.)* a good friend – 31 **outa** *(coll.)* out of

WILLY: Cause I get so lonely – especially when business is bad and there's nobody to talk to. I get the feeling that I'll never sell anything again, that I won't make a living for you, or a business, a business for the boys. *(He talks through The Woman's subsiding laughter; The Woman primps at the "mirror.")* There's so much I want to make for …

THE WOMAN: Me? You didn't make me, Willy. I picked you.

WILLY *(pleased)*: You picked me?

THE WOMAN: *(who is quite proper-looking, Willy's age)*: I did. I've been sitting at that desk watching all the salesmen go by, day in, day out. But you've got such a sense of humor, and we do have such a good time together, don't we?

WILLY: Sure, sure. *(He takes her in his arms.)* Why do you have to go now?

THE WOMAN: It's two o'clock …

WILLY: No, come on in! *(He pulls her.)*

THE WOMAN:… my sisters'll be scandalized. When'll you be back?

WILLY: Oh, two weeks about. Will you come up again?

THE WOMAN: Sure thing. You do make me laugh. It's good for me. *(She squeezes his arm, kisses him.)* And I think you're a wonderful man.

WILLY: You picked me, heh?

THE WOMAN: Sure. Because you're so sweet. And such a kidder.

WILLY: Well, I'll see you next time I'm in Boston.

THE WOMAN: I'll put you right through to the buyers.

WILLY *(slapping her bottom)*: Right. Well, bottoms up!

THE WOMAN *(slaps him gently and laughs)*: You just kill me, Willy. *(He suddenly grabs her and kisses her roughly.)* You kill me. And thanks for the stockings. I love a lot of stockings. Well, good night.

WILLY: Good night. And keep your pores open!

THE WOMAN: Oh, Willy!

---

5 **to subside** [–ʹ–] to become quieter – 5 **to primp** to make oneself look tidier – 9 **proper** decent – 17 **to be scandalized** to be shocked because of a scandal – 24 **kidder** a person who likes to tease – 26 **to put sb through** to connect sb with another person – 27 **to slap** to hit with an open hand – 27 **bottom** the part of the body you sit on – 27 **bottoms up** cheers, sth said before drinking an alcoholic drink: drink up as fast as possible so that the bottom of the glass can be turned up;*here:* a play on the word "bottom" – 28 **to kill sb** *(sl.)* to amuse sb very much – 32 **keep your pores open** remain sexually inviting – 32 **pores** small holes in the skin that let out sweat

(The Woman bursts out laughing, and Linda's laughter blends in. The Woman disappears into the dark. Now the area at the kitchen table brightens. Linda is sitting where she was at the kitchen table, but now is mending a pair of her silk stockings.)

5 LINDA: You are, Willy. The handsomest man. You've got no reason to feel that …

WILLY *(coming out of The Woman's dimming area and going over to Linda)*: I'll make it all up to you, Linda, I'll …

LINDA: There's nothing to make up, dear. You're doing fine, bet-
10 ter than …

WILLY *(noticing her mending)*: What's that?

LINDA: Just mending my stockings. They're so expensive …

WILLY *(angrily, taking them from her)*: I won't have you mending stockings in this house! Now throw them out!

15 *(Linda puts the stockings in her pocket.)*

BERNARD *(entering on the run)*: Where is he? If he doesn't study!

WILLY *(moving to the forestage, with great agitation)*: You'll give him the answers!

BERNARD: I do, but I can't on a Regents! That's a state exam!
20 They're liable to arrest me!

WILLY: Where is he? I'll whip him, I'll whip him!

LINDA: And he'd better give back that football, Willy, it's not nice.

WILLY: Biff! Where is he? Why is he taking everything?

25 LINDA: He's too rough with the girls, Willy. All the mothers are afraid of him!

WILLY: I'll whip him!

BERNARD: He's driving the car without a license!

(The Woman's laugh is heard.)

30 WILLY: Shut up!

LINDA: All the mothers …

WILLY: Shut up!

BERNARD *(backing quietly away and out)*: Mr. Birnbaum says he's stuck up.

35 WILLY: Get outa here!

---

1 **to blend in** to combine – 7 **to dim** to become less bright – 8 **to make it up to sb** to do sth for sb to show how sorry you are about how you treated them – 17 **agitation** [– –ʹ– –] anxiety – 20 **liable** [ˈlaɪəbl] likely – 25 **rough** [rʌf] not gentle, violent – 34 **to be stuck up** to have too high an opinion of oneself

BERNARD: If he doesn't buckle down he'll flunk math! *(He goes off.)*

LINDA: He's right, Willy, you've gotta …

WILLY *(exploding at her)*: There's nothing the matter with him!
5   You want him to be a worm like Bernard? He's got spirit, personality …

(As he speaks, Linda, almost in tears, exits into the living room. Willy is alone in the kitchen, wilting and staring. The leaves are gone. It is night again, and the apartment houses look down
10   *from behind.)*

WILLY: Loaded with it. Loaded! What is he stealing? He's giving it back, isn't he? Why is he stealing? What did I tell him? I never in my life told him anything but decent things.

(Happy in pajamas has come down the stairs; Willy suddenly
15   *becomes aware of Happy's presence.)*

HAPPY: Let's go now, come on.

WILLY *(sitting down at the kitchen table)*: Hub! Why did she have to wax the floors herself? Everytime she waxes the floors she keels over. She knows that!

20 HAPPY: Shh! Take it easy. What brought you back tonight?

WILLY: I got an awful scare. Nearly hit a kid in Yonkers. God! Why didn't I go to Alaska with my brother Ben that time! Ben! That man was a genius, that man was success incarnate! What a mistake! He begged me to go.

25 HAPPY: Well, there's no use in …

WILLY: You guys! There was a man started with the clothes on his back and ended up with diamond mines!

HAPPY: Boy, someday I'd like to know how he did it.

WILLY: What's the mystery? The man knew what he wanted and
30   went out and got it! Walked into a jungle, and comes out, the age of twenty-one, and he's rich! The world is an oyster, but you don't crack it open on a mattress!

---

1 **to buckle down** to start working seriously – 4 **to explode** *here:* to suddenly become angry – 8 **wilting** looking tired and defeated – 11 **Loaded with it.** Really full of personality. – 19 **to keel over** to fall over because of shock or too much work – 21 **scare** sudden feeling of being frightened – 23 **success incarnate** [ɪnˈkɑːnət] the very model of success – 31 **The world is an oyster.** The world is yours for the taking. You can achieve anthing if you try hard enough. – 31 **oyster** Auster – 32 **to crack sth open** to open sth by force

HAPPY: Pop, I told you I'm gonna retire you for life.

WILLY: You'll retire me for life on seventy goddam dollars a week? And your women and your car and your apartment, and you'll retire me for life! Christ's sake, I couldn't get past
5 Yonkers today! Where are you guys, where are you? The woods are burning! I can't drive a car!

(Charley has appeared in the doorway. He is a large man, slow of speech, laconic, immovable. In all he says, despite what he says, there is pity, and, now, trepidation. He has a robe over
10 *pajamas, slippers on his feet. He enters the kitchen.)*

CHARLEY: Everything all right?

HAPPY: Yeah, Charley, everything's …

WILLY: What's the matter?

CHARLEY: I heard some noise. I thought something happened.
15 Can't we do something about the walls? You sneeze in here, and in my house hats blow off.

HAPPY: Let's go to bed, Dad. Come on.

(Charley signals to Happy to go.)

WILLY: You go ahead, I'm not tired at the moment.
20 HAPPY *(to* Willy): Take it easy, huh? *(He exits.)*

WILLY: What're you doin' up?

CHARLEY *(sitting down at the kitchen table opposite* Willy): Couldn't sleep good. I had a heartburn.

WILLY: Well, you don't know how to eat.
25 CHARLEY: I eat with my mouth.

WILLY: No, you're ignorant. You gotta know about vitamins and things like that.

CHARLEY: Come on, let's shoot. Tire you out a little.

WILLY *(hesitantly)*: All right. You got cards?
30 CHARLEY: *(taking a deck from his pocket)*: Yeah, I got them. Someplace. What is it with those vitamins?

WILLY *(dealing)*: They build up your bones. Chemistry.

CHARLEY: Yeah, but there's no bones in a heartburn.

---

1 **I'm gonna retire you for life.** I'm going to make it possible for you to stop working for the rest of your life. – 1 **to retire** to stop doing one's job because of reaching a certain age – 4 **Christ's sake!** For Christ's sake! (Du lieber Gott!) – 5 **The woods are burning!** There's a crisis. – 8 **laconic** [lə'kɒnɪk] using few words to express oneself – 9 **trepidation** fear, anxiety – 10 **slippers** loose soft shoes worn in the house – 23 **heartburn** a feeling of burning in the stomach – 28 **let's shoot** let's start, *here:* let's start playing cards – 28 **to tire sb** to make sb tired – 30 **deck** pack of playing cards – 32 **to deal** to pass out cards to the players

WILLY: What are you talkin' about? Do you know the first thing about it?

CHARLEY: Don't get insulted.

WILLY: Don't talk about something you don't know anything
5   about.

(They are playing. Pause.)

CHARLEY: What're you doin' home?

WILLY: A little trouble with the car.

CHARLEY: Oh. *(Pause.)* I'd like to take a trip to California.

10 WILLY: Don't say.

CHARLEY: You want a job?

WILLY: I got a job, I told you that. *(After a slight pause.)* What the hell are you offering me a job for?

CHARLEY: Don't get insulted.

15 WILLY: Don't insult me.

CHARLEY: I don't see no sense in it. You don't have to go on this way.

WILLY: I got a good job. *(Slight pause.)* What do you keep comin' in here for?

20 CHARLEY: You want me to go?

WILLY *(after a pause, withering)*: I can't understand it. He's going back to Texas again. What the hell is that?

CHARLEY: Let him go.

WILLY: I got nothin' to give him, Charley, I'm clean, I'm clean.

25 CHARLEY: He won't starve. None a them starve. Forget about him.

WILLY: Then what have I got to remember?

CHARLEY: You take it too hard. To hell with it. When a deposit bottle is broken you don't get your nickel back.

30 WILLY: That's easy enough for you to say.

CHARLEY: That ain't easy for me to say.

WILLY: Did you see the ceiling I put up in the living room?

CHARLEY: Yeah, that's a piece of work. To put up a ceiling is a mystery to me. How do you do it?

35 WILLY: What's the difference?

CHARLEY: Well, talk about it.

---

1 **the first thing** anything at all – 3 **to insult** [–ˈ–] to say impolite things to a person so as to hurt him – 10 **Don't say.** You don't say. (= Is that right?) – 21 **withering** feeling ashamed or inferior – 24 **I'm clean** . I've got no money – 25 **none a them** *(sl.)* none of them – 28 **a deposit bottle** a bottle for which a small amount of money is paid and the money is given back when the empty bottle is returned – 29 **nickel** American coin worth five cents

WILLY: You gonna put up a ceiling?

CHARLEY: How could I put up a ceiling?

WILLY: Then what the hell are you bothering me for?

CHARLEY: You're insulted again.

5 WILLY: A man who can't handle tools is not a man. You're disgusting.

CHARLEY: Don't call me disgusting, Willy.

(Uncle Ben, carrying a valise and an umbrella, enters the forestage from around the right corner of the house. He is a stolid
10 *man, in his sixties, with a mustache and an authoritative air. He is utterly certain of his destiny, and there is an aura of far places about him. He enters exactly as Willy speaks.)*

WILLY: I'm getting awfully tired, Ben.

(Ben's music is heard. Ben looks around at everything.)

15 CHARLEY: Good, keep playing; you'll sleep better. Did you call me Ben?

(Ben looks at his watch.)

WILLY: That's funny. For a second there you reminded me of my brother Ben.

20 BEN: I only have a few minutes. *(He strolls, inspecting the place. Willy and Charley continue playing.)*

CHARLEY: You never heard from him again, heh? Since that time?

WILLY: Didn't Linda tell you? Couple of weeks ago we got a letter
25 from his wife in Africa. He died.

CHARLEY: That so.

BEN *(chuckling)*: So this is Brooklyn, eh?

CHARLEY: Maybe you're in for some of his money.

WILLY: Naa, he had seven sons. There's just one opportunity I
30 had with that man …

BEN: I must make a train, William. There are several properties I'm looking at in Alaska.

---

5 **disgusting** [–´– –] very unpleasant – 8 **valise** [vəˈliːz] a small traveling bag – 9 **stolid** showing little emotion – 10 **mustache** [ˈmʌstɪʃ] hair growing on the upper lip – 10 **authoritative air** [–´– – – –] appearance of power and importance – 11 **utterly** completely – 11 **destiny** what will happen in the future, fate – 20 **to stroll** to walk at a slow pace – 27 **to chuckle** to laugh quietly – 27 **Brooklyn** part of New York City, mostly residential with a lower middle-class and middle-class population – 28 **to be in for sth** to be going to get sth – 31 **to make a train** to be on time to get a train. – 31 **properties** land, buildings

WILLY: Sure, sure! If I'd gone with him to Alaska that time, everything would've been totally different.

CHARLEY: Go on, you'd froze to death up there.

WILLY: What're you talking about?

5 BEN: Opportunity is tremendous in Alaska, William. Surprised
you're not up there.

WILLY: Sure, tremendous.

CHARLEY: Heh?

WILLY: There was the only man I ever met who knew the
10 answers.

CHARLEY: Who?

BEN: How are you all?

WILLY *(taking a pot, smiling)*: Fine, fine.

CHARLEY: Pretty sharp tonight.

15 BEN: Is Mother living with you?

WILLY: No, she died a long time ago.

CHARLEY: Who?

BEN: That's too bad. Fine specimen of a lady, Mother.

WILLY *(to Charley)*: Heh?

20 BEN: I'd hoped to see the old girl.

CHARLEY: Who died?

BEN: Heard anything from Father, have you?

WILLY *(unnerved)*: What do you mean, who died?

CHARLEY *(taking a pot)*: What're you talkin' about?

25 BEN *(looking at his watch)*: William, it's half past eight!

WILLY *(as though to dispel his confusion he angrily stops Charley's hand)*: That's my build!

CHARLEY: I put the ace …

WILLY: If you don't know how to play the game I'm not gonna
30 throw my money away on you!

CHARLEY: *(rising)*: It was my ace, for God's sake!

WILLY: I'm through, I'm through!

BEN: When did Mother die?

WILLY: Long ago. Since the beginning you never knew how to
35 play cards.

CHARLEY *(picks up the cards and goes to the door)*: All right! Next
time I'll bring a deck with five aces.

WILLY: I don't play that kind of game!

---

3 **Go on!** I don't believe you! – 3 **you'd froze** you would have frozen – 13 **pot** the total
amount of money each player has decided to risk; the winner takes the whole pot –
14 **sharp** *here:* playing well – 18 **specimen** ['spesəmɪn] example – 23 **unnerved** having
lost one's calm – 26 **to dispel** [-'-] to drive away – 27 **build** *here:* set of cards – 28 **ace**
As – 32 **to be through** to have enough of sth, to be finished

CHARLEY *(turning to him)*: You ought to be ashamed of your-self …

WILLY: Yeah?

CHARLEY: Yeah! *(he goes out.)*

5 WILLY *(slamming the door after him)*: Ignoramus!

BEN *(as Willy comes toward him through the wall-line of the kitchen)*: So you're William.

WILLY *(shaking Ben's hand)*: Ben! I've been waiting for you so long! What's the answer? How did you do it?

10 BEN: Oh, there's a story in that.

(Linda enters the forestage, as of old, carrying the wash basket.)

LINDA: Is this Ben?

BEN *(gallantly)*: How do you do, my dear.

15 LINDA: Where've you been all these years? Willy's always wondered why you …

WILLY *(pulling Ben away from her impatiently)*: Where is Dad? Didn't you follow him? How did you get started?

BEN: Well, I don't know how much you remember.

20 WILLY: Well, I was just a baby, of course, only three or four years old …

BEN: Three years and eleven months.

WILLY: What a memory, Ben!

BEN: I have many enterprises, William, and I have never kept
25 books.

WILLY: I remember I was sitting under the wagon in – was it Nebraska?

BEN: It was South Dakota, and I gave you a bunch of wild flowers.

30 WILLY: I remember you walking away down some open road.

BEN *(laughing)*: I was going to find Father in Alaska.

WILLY: Where is he?

BEN: At that age I had a very faulty view of geography, William. I discovered after a few days that I was heading due south, so
35 instead of Alaska, I ended up in Africa.

LINDA: Africa!

WILLY: The Gold Coast!

5 **to slam** to shut th. with force – 5 **Ignoramus!** [ɪgnəˈreɪməs] You stupid person! – 24 **to keep books** to keep written records of the money taken in and spent – 28 **bunch** small group of things usually fastened together – 33 **faulty** imperfect – 34 **due** directly – 37 **the Gold Coast** a coast on the Gulf of Guinea in western Africa

BEN: Principally diamond mines.

LINDA: Diamond mines!

BEN: Yes, my dear. But I've only a few minutes …

WILLY: No! Boys! Boys! *(Young Biff and Happy appear.)* Listen to
5   this. This is your Uncle Ben, a great man! Tell my boys, Ben!

BEN: Why, boys, when I was seventeen I walked into the jungle,
and when I was twenty-one I walked out. *(He laughs.)* And by
God I was rich.

WILLY *(to the boys)*: You see what I been talking about? The
10   greatest things can happen!

BEN *(glancing at his watch)*: I have an appointment in Ketchikan Tuesday week.

WILLY: No, Ben! Please tell about Dad. I want my boys to hear.
I want them to know the kind of stock they spring from. All I
15   remember is a man with a big beard, and I was in Mamma's
lap, sitting around a fire, and some kind of high music.

BEN: His flute. He played the flute.

WILLY: Sure, the flute, that's right! *(New music is heard, a high,
rollicking tune.)*

20 BEN: Father was a very great and a very wild-hearted man. We
would start in Boston, and he'd toss the whole family into the
wagon, and then he'd drive the team right across the country; through Ohio, and Indiana, Michigan, Illinois and all the
Western states. And we'd stop in the towns and sell the flutes
25   that he'd made on the way. Great inventor, Father. With one
gadget he made more in a week than a man like you could
make in a lifetime.

WILLY: That's just the way I'm bringing them up, Ben – rugged,
well liked, all-around.

30 BEN: Yeah? *(To Biff.)* Hit that, boy – hard as you can. *(He pounds
his stomach.)*

BIFF: Oh, no, sir!

BEN *(taking boxing stance)*: Come on, get to me! *(He laughs)*

WILLY: Go to it, Biff! Go ahead, show him!

---

1 **principally** for the most part – 11 **to glance at sth** to take a quick look at sth –
11 **appointment** an arrangement to meet sb at a certain time – 11 **Ketchikan** ['ketʃəkən]
city in southeast Alaska – 14 **stock** family – 14 **to spring from** *here:* to be descended
from – 16 **lap** Schoß – 16 **high** with high notes – 19 **rollicking tune** lively and merry
melody – 21 **to toss** *here:* to quickly put – 26 **gadget** small useful device – 28 **rugged**
['rʌgɪd] determined, not easily upset, but honest – 29 **all-around** [ˌ–'–] good at many
different things – 33 **stance** position, way of standing – 33 **get to me** try to hit me

BIFF: Okay! *(He cocks his fists and starts in.)*
LINDA *(to Willy)*: Why must he fight, dear?
BEN *(sparring with Biff)*: Good boy! Good boy!
WILLY: How's that, Ben, heh?

5 HAPPY: Give him the left, Biff!
LINDA: Why are you fighting?
BEN: Good boy! *(Suddenly comes in, trips Biff, and stands over him, the point of his umbrella poised over Biff's eye.)*
LINDA: Look out, Biff!

10 BIFF: Gee!
BEN *(Patting Biff's knee)*: Never fight fair with a stranger, boy. You'll never get out of the jungle that way. *(Taking Linda's hand and bowing.)* It was an honor and a pleasure to meet you, Linda.

15 LINDA *(withdrawing her hand coldly, frightened)*: Have a nice – trip.
BEN *(to Willy)*: And good luck with your – what do you do?
WILLY: Selling.
BEN: Yes. Well … *(He raises his hand in farewell to all.)*

20 WILLY: No, Ben, I don't want you to think … *(He takes Ben's arm to show him)* It's Brooklyn, I know, but we hunt too.
BEN: Really, now.
WILLY: Oh, sure, there's snakes and rabbits and – that's why I moved out here. Why Biff can fell any one of these trees in
25 no time. Boys! Go right over to where they're building the apartment house and get some sand. We're gonna rebuild the entire front stoop right now! Watch this, Ben!
BIFF: Yes, sir! On the double, Hap!
HAPPY *(as he and Biff run off)*: I lost weight, Pop, you notice?

30 *(Charley enters in knickers, even before the boys are gone.)*

CHARLEY: Listen, if they steal any more from that building the watchman'll put the cops on them!
LINDA *(to Willy)*: Don't let Biff …

---

1 **to cock one's fists** to put up one's fists into fighting position – 1 **to start in** *here:* to get in close to the other person – 3 **to spar** to box with gentle blows to test the opponent or to train in boxing – 5 **Give him the left** Hit him with your left fist – 7 **to trip** to cause sb to fall down – 8 **poised** [pɔɪzd] held in position ready to be used at – any second 13 **to bow** [baʊ] to bend the body down as a formal way of greeting sb – 15 **to withdraw** [-'-] to take away – 19 **in farewell** as a sign meaning good-bye – 24 **to fell** to cut down – 27 **stoop** porch, veranda – 32 **watchman** ['- -] person who guards property – 32 **to put the cops on sb** *(coll.)* to tell the police to arrest sb

(Ben laughs lustily.)

WILLY: You shoulda seen the lumber they brought home last week. At least a dozen six-by-tens worth all kinds a money.

CHARLEY: Listen, if that watchman …

5　WILLY: I gave them hell, understand. But I got a couple of fearless characters there.

CHARLEY: Willy, the jails are full of fearless characters.

BEN *(clapping Willy on the back, with a laugh at Charley)*: And the stock exchange, friend!

10　WILLY *(joining in Ben's laughter)*: Where are the rest of your pants?

CHARLEY: My wife bought them.

WILLY: Now all you need is a golf club and you can go upstairs and go to sleep. *(To Ben.)* Great athlete! Between him and his

15　son Bernard they can't hammer a nail!

BERNARD *(rushing in)*: The watchman's chasing Biff!

WILLY *(angrily)*: Shut up! He's not stealing anything!

LINDA *(alarmed, hurrying off left)*: Where is he? Biff, dear! *(She exits.)*

20　WILLY *(moving toward the left, away from Ben)*: There's nothing wrong. What's the matter with you?

BEN: Nervy boy. Good!

WILLY *(laughing)*: Oh, nerves of iron, that Biff!

CHARLEY: Don't know what it is. My New England man comes

25　back and he's bleedin', they murdered him up there.

WILLY: It's contacts, Charley, I got important contacts!

CHARLEY *(sarcastically)*: Glad to hear it, Willy. Come in later, we'll shoot a little casino. I'll take some of your Portland money. *(He laughs at Willy and exits.)*

30　WILLY *(turning to Ben)*: Business is bad, it's murderous. But not for me, of course.

BEN: I'll stop by on my way back to Africa.

WILLY *(longingly)*: Can't you stay a few days? You're just what I need, Ben, because I – I have a fine position here, but I – well,

---

1 **lustily** lively, full of strength – 2 **shoulda** *(sl.)* should have – 2 **lumber** wood used for building – 3 **six-by-tens** pieces of wood six inches by ten inches – 8 **to clap** to hit sth lightly with an open hand – 9 **stock exchange** Börse – 11 **pants** trousers – 14 **Between him and his son** … Neither he nor his son … – 22 **nervy** being ready to take risks, bold – 25 **to bleed** to lose blood,*here:* to be in very bad shape – 25 **to murder sb** *here:* to cause sb to be a complete failure – 26 **contacts** people who can help you to be successful – 28 **to shoot** *here:* to play – 28 **casino** [–'– –] a card game – 28 **Portland money** the money earned in Portland – 33 **longingly** with great desire

Dad left when I was such a baby and I never had a chance to talk to him and I still feel – kind of temporary about myself.

BEN: I'll be late for my train.

(They are at opposite ends of the stage.)

5 WILLY: Ben, my boys – can't we talk? They'd go into the jaws of hell for me, see, but I …

BEN: William, you're being first-rate with your boys. Outstanding, manly chaps!

WILLY *(hanging on to his words)*: Oh, Ben, that's good to hear!
10 Because sometimes I'm afraid that I'm not teaching them the right kind of – Ben, how should I teach them?

BEN *(giving great weight to each word, and with a certain vicious audacity)*: William, when I walked into the jungle, I was seventeen. When I walked out I was twenty-one. And, by God, I
15 was rich! *(He goes off into darkness around the right corner of the house.)*

WILLY: … was rich! That's just the spirit I want to imbue them with! To walk into a jungle! I was right! I was right! I was right!

20 *(Ben is gone, but Willy is still speaking to him as Linda, in nightgown and robe, enters the kitchen, glances around for Willy, then goes to the door of the house, looks out and sees him. Comes down to his left. He looks at her.)*

LINDA: Willy, dear? Willy?

25 WILLY: I was right!

LINDA: Did you have some cheese? *(He can't answer.)* It's very late, darling. Come to bed, heh?

WILLY *(looking straight up)*: Gotta break your neck to see a star in this yard.

30 LINDA: You coming in?

WILLY: Whatever happened to that diamond watch fob? Remember? When Ben came from Africa that time? Didn't he give me a watch fob with a diamond in it?

---

2 **temporary** not settled, not fulfilled – 5 **They'd go into the jaws of hell for me.** They would do almost anything for me. – 5 **jaws** [dʒɔːz] Rachen – 7 **to be first-rate** *here:* to do an excellent job – 8 **manly** masculine, strong, aggressive – 12 **vicious** ['vɪʃəs] brutal, cruel – 13 **audacity** [ɔːˈdɛsɪti] boldness, daring – 17 **to imbue** to fill – 21 **nightgown** dress worn by women in bed – 28 **gotta** *(sl.)* you have (got) to – 31 **fob** short chain attached to a pocket watch

LINDA: You pawned it, dear. Twelve, thirteen years ago. For Biff's radio correspondence course.

WILLY: Gee that was a beautiful thing. I'll take a walk.

LINDA: But you're in your slippers.

5 WILLY *(starting to go around the house at the left)*: I was right! I was! *(Half to Linda, as he goes, shaking his head.)* What a man! There was a man worth talking to. I was right!

LINDA *(calling after Willy)*: But in your slippers, Willy!

(Willy is almost gone when Biff, in his pajamas, comes down
10 *the stairs and enters the kitchen.)*

BIFF: What is he doing out there?

LINDA: Sh!

BIFF: God Almighty. Mom, how long has he been doing this?

LINDA: Don't, he'll hear you.

15 BIFF: What the hell is the matter with him?

LINDA: It'll pass by morning.

BIFF: Shouldn't we do anything?

LINDA: Oh, my dear, you should do a lot of things, but there's nothing to do, so go to sleep.

20 *(Happy comes down the stair and sits on the steps.)*

HAPPY: I never heard him so loud, Mom.

LINDA: Well, come around more often; you'll hear him. *(She sits down at the table and mends the lining of Willy's jacket.)*

BIFF: Why didn't you ever write me about this, Mom?

25 LINDA: How would I write to you? For over three months you had no address.

BIFF: I was on the move. But you know I thought of you all the time. You know that, don't you, pal?

LINDA: I know, dear, I know. But he likes to have a letter. Just to
30 know that there's still a possibility for better things.

BIFF: He's not like this all the time, is he?

LINDA: It's when you come home he's always the worst.

BIFF: When I come home?

LINDA: When you write you're coming, he's all smiles, and talks
35 about the future, and – he's just wonderful. And then the closer you seem to come, the more shaky he gets, and then,

---

1 **to pawn** to give as security for the payment of money borrowed (verpfänden) – 2 **correspondence course** a course in which one studies at home: instruction, tests etc. are sent by mail – 16 **It'll pass** ... It (Willy's strange, behavior) will go away... – 23 **lining** material on the inside of a coat or jacket – 27 **on the move** constantly traveling – 34 **he's all smiles** he's very happy – 36 **shaky** anxious, nervous

by the time you get here, he's arguing, and he seems angry at you. I think it's just that maybe he can't bring himself to – to open up to you. Why are you so hateful to each other? Why is that?

5 BIFF *(evasively)*: I'm not hateful, Mom.

LINDA: But you no sooner come in the door than you're fighting!

BIFF: I don't know why. I mean to change. I'm tryin', Mom, you understand?

10 LINDA: Are you home to stay now?

BIFF: I don't know. I want to look around, see what's doin'.

LINDA: Biff, you can't look around all your life, can you?

BIFF: I just can't take hold, Mom. I can't take hold of some kind of a life.

15 LINDA: Biff, a man is not a bird, to come and go with the springtime.

BIFF: Your hair … *(He touches her hair.)* Your hair got so gray.

LINDA: Oh, it's been gray since you were in high school. I just stopped dyeing it, that's all.

20 BIFF: Dye it again, will ya? I don't want my pal looking old. *(He smiles.)*

LINDA: You're such a boy! You think you can go away for a year and… You've got to get it into your head now that one day you'll knock on this door and there'll be strange people
25 here …

BIFF: What are you talking about? You're not even sixty, Mom.

LINDA: But what about your father?

BIFF *(lamely)*: Well, I meant him too.

HAPPY: He admires Pop.

30 LINDA: Biff, dear, if you don't have any feeling for him, then you can't have any feeling for me.

BIFF: Sure I can, Mom.

LINDA: No. You can't just come to see me, because I love him. *(With a threat, but only a threat, of tears.)* He's the dearest
35 man in the world to me, and I won't have anyone making him feel unwanted and low and blue. You've got to make up your mind now, darling, there's no leeway any more. Either he's

---

2 **to bring oneself to do sth** to make oneself do sth unpleasant – 2 **to open up to sb** to tell sb how you really feel about sth – 5 **evasively** [ɪˈveɪsɪvli] trying to avoid answering a question directly – 11 **what's doin'** *(coll.)* what's going on – 13 **I can't take hold of some kind of a life.** I can't find anything that will give my life direction and meaning. – 13 **to take hold** to find sth that is lasting and meaningful – 19 **to dye** [daɪ] to give sth a new color – 20 **ya** *(sl.)* you – 28 **lamely** unconvincingly (nicht überzeugend) – 36 **low** depressed – 36 **blue** sad – 37 **leeway** freedom of action

your father and you pay him that respect, or else you're not to come here. I know he's not easy to get along with – nobody knows that better than me – but …

WILLY *(from the left, with a laugh)*: Hey, hey, Biffo!

5 BIFF *(starting to go out after* Willy): What the hell is the matter with him?

(Happy stops him.)

LINDA: Don't – don't go near him!

BIFF: Stop making excuses for him! He always, always wiped the
10 floor with you. Never had an ounce of respect for you.

HAPPY: He's always had respect for …

BIFF: What the hell do you know about it?

HAPPY *(surlily)*: Just don't call him crazy!

BIFF: He's got no character – Charley wouldn't do this. Not in his
15 own house – spewing out that vomit from his mind.

HAPPY: Charley never had to cope with what he's got to.

BIFF: People are worse off than Willy Loman. Believe me, I've seen them!

LINDA: Then make Charley your father, Biff. You can't do that,
20 can you? I don't say he's a great man. Willy Loman never made a lot of money. His name was never in the paper. He's not the finest character that ever lived. But he's a human being, and a terrible thing is happening to him. So attention must be paid. He's not to be allowed to fall into his grave like an old dog.
25 Attention, attention must be finally paid to such a person. You called him crazy …

BIFF: I didn't mean …

LINDA: No, a lot of people think he's lost his – balance. But you don't have to be very smart to know what his trouble is. The
30 man is exhausted.

HAPPY: Sure!

LINDA: A small man can be just as exhausted as a great man. He works for a company thirty-six years this March, opens up

---

1 **you pay him that respect** you respect him for that – 9 **to wipe the floor with sb** to be domineering, to treat sb disrespectfully – 10 **Never had an ounce of respect for you.** He never had even a little bit of respect for you. – 10 **ounce** [auns] small unit of weight (28 grams) – 13 **surlily** ['sɜːlɪli] angrily, rudely – 15 **to spew** [spjuː] to force out in large amounts – 15 **spewing out that vomit** ['vɒmɪt] saying all that nonsense – 15 **vomit** ['vɒmɪt] food that has been eaten and is then forced out of the mouth from the stomach – 16 **to cope with sth** to put up with sth – 17 **to be worse off** to be in an even worse situation – 28 **to lose one's balance** to become crazy

unheard-of territories to their trademark, and now in his old age they take his salary away.

HAPPY *(indignantly)*: I didn't know that, Mom.

LINDA: You never asked, my dear! Now that you get your spend-
5   ing money someplace else you don't trouble your mind with him.

HAPPY: But I gave you money last …

LINDA: Christmas time, fifty dollars! To fix the hot water it cost ninety-seven fifty! For five weeks he's been on straight com-
10   mission, like a beginner, an unknown!

BIFF: Those ungrateful bastards!

LINDA: Are they any worse than his sons? When he brought them business, when he was young, they were glad to see him. But now his old friends, the old buyers that loved him so
15   and always found some order to hand him in a pinch – they're all dead, retired. He used to be able to make six, seven calls a day in Boston. Now he takes his valises out of the car and puts them back and takes them out again and he's exhausted. Instead of walking he talks now. He drives seven hundred
20   miles, and when he gets there no one knows him any more, no one welcomes him. And what goes through a man's mind, driving seven hundred miles home without having earned a cent? Why shouldn't he talk to himself? Why? When he has to go to Charley and borrow fifty dollars a week and pretend to
25   me that it's his pay? How long can that go on? How long? You see what I'm sitting here and waiting for? And you tell me he has no character? The man who never worked a day but for your benefit? When does he get the medal for that? Is this his reward – to turn around at the age of sixty-three and find his
30   sons, who he loved better than his life, one a philandering bum…

HAPPY: Mom!

LINDA: That's all you are, my baby! *(To Biff.)* And you! What happened to the love you had for him? You were such pals! How
35   you used to talk to him on the phone every night! How lonely he was till he could come home to you!

---

1 **trademark** name or symbol used by a manufacturer – 3 **indignantly** [–ˈ– – –] angrily because one feels one has been treated unfairly – 8 **to fix** to repair – 9 **to be on straight commission** to have no regular salary, to earn only a percentage of what one sells – 15 **in a pinch** in a situation of great need – 28 **benefit** [ˈbenɪfɪt] advantage – 28 **medal** small metal prize given to reward achievement;*here:* recognition – 30 **to philander** to have a lot of casual love affairs with women – 31 **bum** worthless person, good-for-nothing

BIFF: All right, Mom. I'll live here in my room, and I'll get a job. I'll keep away from him, that's all.

LINDA: No, Biff. You can't stay here and fight all the time.

BIFF: He threw me out of this house, remember that.

5 LINDA: Why did he do that? I never knew why.

BIFF: Because I know he's a fake and he doesn't like anybody around who knows!

LINDA: Why a fake? In what way? What do you mean?

BIFF: Just don't lay it all at my feet. It's between me and him
10 – that's all I have to say. I'll chip in from now on. He'll settle for half my pay check. He'll be all right. I'm going to bed. *(He starts for the stairs.)*

LINDA: He won't be all right.

BIFF *(turning on the stairs, furiously)*: I hate this city and I'll stay
15 here. Now what do you want?

LINDA: He's dying, Biff.

(Happy turns quickly to her, shocked.)

BIFF *(after a pause)*: Why is he dying?

LINDA: He's been trying to kill himself.

20 BIFF *(with great horror)*: How?

LINDA: I live from day to day.

BIFF: What're you talking about?

LINDA: Remember I wrote you that he smashed up the car again? In February?

25 BIFF: Well?

LINDA: The insurance inspector came. He said that they have evidence. That all these accidents in the last year – weren't – weren't – accidents.

HAPPY: How can they tell that? That's a lie.

30 LINDA: It seems there's a woman … *(She takes a breath as)*

BIFF *(sharply but contained)*: What woman?

LINDA *(simultaneously)*: … and this woman …

LINDA: What?

BIFF: Nothing. Go ahead.

35 LINDA: What did you say?

---

6 **a fake** sb or sth that isn't what it seems to be – 9 … **don't lay it all at my feet.** … don't make me responsible for everything. – 10 **to chip in** to help out by contributing some money – 10 **to settle for sth** to accept sth in spite of not being completely satisfied – 11 **pay check** *here:* wages – 26 **insurance** [ɪnˈʃʊərəns] Versicherung – 26 **insurance inspector** person from an insurance company who makes sure nobody is trying to get money from the company dishonestly – 27 **evidence** [ˈevɪdəns] anything that can show that sth is true – 31 **contained** *here:* in control of his emotions

BIFF: Nothing, I just said what woman?

HAPPY: What about her?

LINDA: Well, it seems she was walking down the road and saw his car. She says that he wasn't driving fast at all, and that he
5 didn't skid. She says he came to that little bridge, and then deliberately smashed into the railing, and it was only the shallowness of the water that saved him.

BIFF: Oh, no, he probably just fell asleep again.

LINDA: I don't think he fell asleep.

10 BIFF: Why not?

LINDA: Last month ... *(With great difficulty.)* Oh, boys, it's so hard to say a thing like this! He's just a big stupid man to you, but I tell you there's more good in him than in many other people. *(She chokes, wipes her eyes.)* I was looking for a fuse.
15 The lights blew out, and I went down the cellar. And behind the fuse box – it happened to fall out – was a length of rubber pipe – just short.

HAPPY: No kidding!

LINDA: There's a little attachment on the end of it. I knew right
20 away. And sure enough, on the bottom of the water heater there's a new little nipple on the gas pipe.

HAPPY *(angrily)*: That – jerk.

BIFF: Did you have it taken off?

LINDA: I'm – I'm ashamed to. How can I mention it to him? Every
25 day I go down and take away that little rubber pipe. But, when he comes home, I put it back where it was. How can I insult him that way? I don't know what to do. I live from day to day, boys. I tell you, I know every thought in his mind. It sounds so old-fashioned and silly, but I tell you he put his whole life into
30 you and you've turned your backs on him. *(She is bent over in the chair, weeping, her face in her hands.)* Biff, I swear to God! Biff, his life is in your hands!

HAPPY *(to Biff)*: How do you like that damned fool!

---

5 **to skid** to slip or slide usually when it is wet or icy – 6 **deliberately** on purpose –
7 **shallowness** [ˈʃæləʊnəs] state of not being very deep – 14 **to choke** to pause to take a
breath when on the point of crying – 14 **fuse** Sicherung – 16 **a length** a piece – 17 **pipe**
tube through which gas, water, etc. can flow – 18 **No kidding?** Are you sure what you're
saying is true? – 19 **attachment** sth that makes it possible to connect one thing to
another – 20 **sure enough** as could be expected – 21 **nipple** a small opening that sticks
out to which a tube or pipe can be connected – 22 **jerk** *(sl.)* foolish or stupid person –
33 **How do you like that damned fool!** What a stupid man he is!

BIFF *(kissing her)*: All right, pal, all right. It's all settled now. I've been remiss. I know that, Mom. But now I'll stay, and I swear to you, I'll apply myself *(Kneeling in front of her, in a fever of self-reproach.)* It's just – you see, Mom, I don't fit in business.
5   Not that I won't try. I'll try, and I'll make good.

HAPPY: Sure you will. The trouble with you in business was you never tried to please people.

BIFF: I know, I …

HAPPY: Like when you worked for Harrison's. Bob Harrison said
10   you were tops, and then you go and do some damn fool thing like whistling whole songs in the elevator like a comedian.

BIFF *(against Happy)*: So what? I like to whistle sometimes.

HAPPY: You don't raise a guy to a responsible job who whistles in the elevator!

15 LINDA: Well, don't argue about it now.

HAPPY: Like when you'd go off and swim in the middle of the day instead of taking the line around.

BIFF *(his resentment rising)*: Well, don't you run off? You take off sometimes, don't you? On a nice summer day?

20 HAPPY: Yeah, but I cover myself.

LINDA: Boys!

HAPPY: If I'm going to take a fade the boss can call any number where I'm supposed to be and they'll swear to him that I just left. I'll tell you something that I hate so say, Biff, but in the
25   business world some of them think you're crazy.

BIFF *(angered)*: Screw the business world!

HAPPY: All right, screw it! Great, but cover yourself!

LINDA: Hap, Hap.

BIFF: I don't care what they think! They've laughed at Dad for
30   years, and you know why? Because we don't belong in this nuthouse of a city! We should be mixing cement on some open plain or – or carpenters. A carpenter is allowed to whistle!

---

1 **It's all settled now.** It's clear what must be done. – 2 **to be remiss** [rɪ'mɪs] to be careless, to not take care of one's responsibilities – 3 **to apply oneself** to work harder and with more effort and concentration – 3 **in a fever of self-reproach** emotionally blaming himself for not having done enough – 4 **self-reproach** blaming oneself for sth – 5 **to make good** to be successful, to make up for disappointing behavior in the past – 10 **tops** *(sl.)* excellent – 12 **So what?** What's wrong with that? – 17 **to take the line around** to visit customers and show them the range of products – 18 **resentment** a feeling of anger because of being badly treated – 20 **to cover oneself** to make arrangements so that what one is doing is not discovered – 22 **to take a fade** *(sl.)* to be absent for a short time – 26 **Screw the business world!** The business world can go to hell! – 31 **nuthouse** ['– –] *(sl.)* mental hospital – 31 **open plain** large area of flat land as in the West

(Willy walks in from the entrance of the house, at left.)

WILLY: Even your grandfather was better than a carpenter. *(Pause. They watch him.)* You never grew up. Bernard does not whistle in the elevator, I assure you.

5 BIFF *(as though to laugh Willy out of it)*: Yeah, but you do, Pop.

WILLY: I never in my life whistled in an elevator! And who in the business world thinks I'm crazy?

BIFF: I didn't mean it like that, Pop. Now don't make a whole thing out of it, will ya?

10 WILLY: Go back to the West! Be a carpenter, a cowboy, enjoy yourself!

LINDA: Willy, he was just saying …

WILLY: I heard what he said!

HAPPY *(trying to quiet Willy)*: Hey, Pop, come on now …

15 WILLY *(continuing over Happy's line)*: They laugh at me, heh? Go to Filene's, go to the Hub, go to Slattery's, Boston. Call out the name Willy Loman and see what happens! Big shot!

BIFF: All right, Pop.

WILLY: Big!

20 BIFF: All right!

WILLY: Why do you always insult me?

BIFF: I didn't say a word. *(To Linda.)* Did I say a word?

LINDA: He didn't say anything, Willy.

WILLY *(going to the doorway of the living room)*: All right, good
25 night, good night.

LINDA: Willy, dear, he just decided …

WILLY *(to Biff)* If you get tired hanging around tomorrow, paint the ceiling I put up in the living room.

BIFF: I'm leaving early tomorrow.

30 HAPPY: He's going to see Bill Oliver, Pop.

WILLY *(interestedly)*: Oliver? For what?

BIFF *(with reserve, but trying, trying)*: He always said he'd stake me. I'd like to go into business, so maybe I can take him up on it.

35 LINDA: Isn't that wonderful?

---

5 to laugh sb out of sth to laugh so as to help an angry person forget his/her anger –
8 don't make a whole thing out of it don't make it more serious than it is – 16 **Filene's**
[faɪ'liːnz], **Slatterly's** names of large department stores – 16 **the Hub** the center of
Boston – 17 **big shot** *(sl.)* important person or sb who thinks he is important – 27 **to
hang around** to spend time doing nothing important – 32 **with reserve** keeping back
one's feelings – 32 **to stake sb** to give sb money to start a business – 33 **to take sb up
on sth** to accept an offer sb has made

WILLY: Don't interrupt. What's wonderful about it? There's fifty men in the City of New York who'd stake him. *(To Biff.)* Sporting goods?

BIFF: I guess so. I know something about it and …

5 WILLY: He knows something about it! You know sporting goods better than Spalding, for God's sake! How much is he giving you?

BIFF: I don't know, I didn't even see him yet, but …

WILLY: Then what're you talkin' about?

10 BIFF *(getting angry)*: Well, all I said was I'm gonna see him, that's all!

WILLY *(turning away)*: Ah, you're counting your chickens again.

BIFF: *(starting left for the stairs.)*: Oh, Jesus, I'm going to sleep!

15 WILLY *(calling after him)*: Don't curse in this house!

BIFF *(turning)*: Since when did you get so clean?

HAPPY *(trying to stop them)*: Wait a …

WILLY: Don't use that language to me! I won't have it!

HAPPY *(grabbing Biff, shouts)*: Wait a minute! I got an idea. I got

20 a feasible idea. Come here, Biff, let's talk this over now, let's talk some sense here. When I was down in Florida last time, I thought of a great idea to sell sporting goods. It just came back to me. You and I, Biff – we have a line, the Loman Line. We train a couple of weeks, and put on a couple of exhibi-

25 tions, see?

WILLY: That's an idea!

HAPPY: Wait! We form two basketball teams, see? Two water-polo teams. We play each other. It's a million dollars' worth of publicity. Two brothers, see? The Loman Brothers. Displays in the

30 Royal Palms – all the hotels. And banners over the ring and the basketball court: "Loman Brothers." Baby, we could sell sporting goods!

WILLY: That is a one-million-dollar idea!

LINDA: Marvelous!

35 BIFF: I'm in great shape as far as that's concerned.

HAPPY: And the beauty of it is, Biff, it wouldn't be like a business. We'd be out playin' ball again …

---

2 **sporting goods** sports equipment – 6 **Spalding** a firm that manufactures sports equipment – 12 **to count one's chickens** to make plans or anticipate sth will happen before one can be sure it will (from the saying: Don't count your chickens before they're hatched.) – 15 **to curse** to use words like "Jesus!" to express anger – 16 **clean** *here:* careful about cursing – 20 **feasible** able to be done, possible – 29 **display** [-'-] show, exhibition – 30 **ring** the area in which boxing matches take place – 35 **shape** condition – 36 **And the beauty of it is …** The great thing about it is …

BIFF *(enthused)*: Yeah, that's …

WILLY: Million-dollar …

HAPPY: And you wouldn't get fed up with it, Biff. It'd be the family again. There'd be the old honor, and comradeship, and if
5 you wanted to go off for a swim or somethin' – well, you'd do it! Without some smart cooky gettin' up ahead of you!

WILLY: Lick the world! You guys together could absolutely lick the civilized world.

BIFF: I'll see Oliver tomorrow. Hap, if we could work that out …
10 LINDA: Maybe things are beginning to …

WILLY *(wildly enthused, to Linda)*: Stop interrupting! *(To Biff.)* But don't wear sport jacket and slacks when you see Oliver.

BIFF: No, I'll …

WILLY: A business suit, and talk as little as possible, and don't
15 crack any jokes.

BIFF: He did like me. Always liked me.

LINDA: He loved you!

WILLY *(to Linda)*: Will you stop! *(To Biff.)* Walk in very serious. You are not applying for a boy's job. Money is to pass. Be
20 quiet, fine, and serious. Everybody likes a kidder, but nobody lends him money.

HAPPY: I'll try to get some myself, Biff. I'm sure I can.

WILLY: I see great things for you kids, I think your troubles are over. But remember, start big and you'll end big. Ask for fif
25 teen. How much you gonna ask for?

BIFF: Gee, I don't know …

WILLY: And don't say "Gee." "Gee" is a boy's word. A man walking in for fifteen thousand dollars does not say "Gee!"

BIFF: Ten, I think, would be top though.
30 WILLY: Don't be so modest. You always started too low. Walk in with a big laugh. Don't look worried. Start off with a couple of your good stories to lighten things up. It's not what you say, it's how you say it – because personality always wins the day.

LINDA: Oliver always thought the highest of him …
35 WILLY: Will you let me talk?

BIFF: Don't yell at her, Pop, will ya?

WILLY *(angrily)*: I was talking, wasn't I?

---

1 **enthused** filled with enthusiasm – 3 **to get fed up with sth** to be bored or tired of doing sth – 4 **comradeship** ['– – –] close friendship – 6 **cooky** *(sl.)* person – 7 **to lick** to defeat easily – 12 **slacks** casual trousers – 15 **to crack a joke** to tell a joke – 19 **Money is to pass.** Money is going to pass from one person to another. – 29 **top** the most – 32 **to lighten things up** to make the atmosphere more cheerful and relaxed

BIFF: I don't like you yelling at her all the time, and I'm tellin' you, that's all.

WILLY: What're you, takin' over this house?

LINDA: Willy …

5   WILLY *(turning to her)*: Don't take his side all the time, goddammit!

BIFF *(furiously)*: Stop yelling at her!

WILLY *(suddenly pulling on his cheek, beaten down, guilt ridden)*: Give my best to Bill Oliver – he may remember me. *(He*
10 *exits through the living room doorway.)*

LINDA *(her voice subdued)*: What'd you have to start that for? *(Biff turns away.)* You see how sweet he was as soon as you talked hopefully? *(She goes over to Biff.)* Come up and say good night to him. Don't let him go to bed that way.

15 HAPPY: Come on, Biff, let's buck him up.

LINDA: Please, dear. Just say good night. It takes so little to make him happy. Come. *(She goes through the living room doorway, calling upstairs from within the living room.)* Your pajamas are hanging in the bathroom, Willy!

20 HAPPY *(looking toward where Linda went out)*: What a woman! They broke the mold when they made her. You know that, Biff?

BIFF: He's off salary. My God, working on commission!

HAPPY: Well, let's face it: he's no hot-shot selling man. Except
25 that sometimes, you have to admit, he's a sweet personality.

BIFF *(deciding)*: Lend me ten bucks, will ya? I want to buy some new ties.

HAPPY: I'll take you to a place I know. Beautiful stuff. Wear one of my striped shirts tomorrow.

30 BIFF: She got gray. Mom got awful old. Gee, I'm gonna go in to Oliver tomorrow and knock him for a …

HAPPY: Come on up. Tell that to Dad. Let's give him a whirl. Come on.

BIFF *(steamed up)*: You know, with ten thousand bucks, boy!

---

8 **guilt ridden** aware of having done sth wrong – 11 **subdued** quiet, sad – 15 **to buck sb up** to make sb feel more confident and happy – 21 **to break the mold** to make sth unique that can never be reproduced again (**mold** = a hollow form used to give a particular shape to sth in a molten state) – 23 **to be off salary** to no longer earn a salary – 23 **to work on commission** to earn money from a percentage of the sales only – 24 **let's face it** let's admit the truth – 24 **hot-shot** *(sl.)* great, fantastic – 26 **bucks** *(sl.)* dollars – 31 **knock him for a …** knock him for a loop, impress him – 32 **Let's give him a whirl.** Let's give him sth to get excited about. – 34 **steamed up** excited

HAPPY *(as they go into the living room)*: That's the talk, Biff, that's the first time I've heard the old confidence out of you! *(From within the living room, fading off.)* You're gonna live with me, kid, and any babe you want just say the word …

5 *(The last lines are hardly heard. They are mounting the stairs to their parents' bedroom.)*

LINDA *(entering her bedroom and addressing Willy, who is in the bathroom. She is straightening the bed for him)*: Can you do anything about the shower? It drips.

10 WILLY *(from the bathroom)*: All of a sudden everything falls to pieces. Goddam plumbing, oughta be sued, those people. I hardly finished putting it in and the thing… *(His words rumble off.)*

LINDA: I'm just wondering if Oliver will remember him. You
15 think he might?

WILLY *(coming out of the bathroom in his pajamas)*: Remember him? What's the matter with you, you crazy? If he'd've stayed with Oliver he'd be on top by now! Wait'll Oliver gets a look at him. You don't know the average caliber any more. The aver-
20 age young man today – *(he is getting into bed)* – is got a caliber of zero. Greatest thing in the world for him was to bum around.

(Biff and Happy enter the bedroom. Slight pause.)

WILLY *(stops short, looking at Biff)*: Glad to hear it, boy.
25 HAPPY: He wanted to say good night to you, sport.
WILLY *(to Biff)*: Yeah. Knock him dead, boy. What'd you want to tell me?
BIFF: Just take it easy, Pop. Good night. *(He turns to go.)*
WILLY *(unable to resist)*: And if anything falls off the desk while
30 you're talking to him – like a package or something – don't you pick it up. They have office boys for that.
LINDA: I'll make a big breakfast …
WILLY: Will you let me finish? *(To Biff.)* Tell him you were in the business in the West. Not farm work.
35 BIFF: All right, Dad.

---

4 **babe** *(sl.)* woman – 9 **to drip** to fall in drops even when shut off – 11 **plumbing** ['plʌmɪŋ] system of water pipes in a house – 11 **to sue** [suː] to take sb to court because of unfair treatment – 12 **to rumble off** to continue in a low voice which can barely be heard – 19 **caliber** ['kælɪbə] *here:* ability, intelligence – 20 **is got** *(sl.)* has got – 21 **to bum around** to travel around with no steady job – 25 **sport** *(sl.)* form of address for a person one is fond of

LINDA: I think everything …

WILLY *(going right through her speech)*: And don't undersell
yourself. No less than fifteen thousand dollars.

BIFF *(unable to bear him)*: Okay. Good night, Mom. *(He starts
5   moving.)*

WILLY: Because you got a greatness in you, Biff, remember that.
You got all kinds a greatness … *(He lies back, exhausted. Biff
walks out.)*

LINDA *(calling after Biff)*: Sleep well, darling!

10 HAPPY: I'm gonna get married, Mom. I wanted to tell you.

LINDA: Go to sleep, dear.

HAPPY *(going)*: I just wanted to tell you.

WILLY: Keep up the good work. *(Happy exits.)* God … remember
that Ebbets Field game? The championship of the city?

15 LINDA: Just rest. Should I sing to you?

WILLY: Yeah. Sing to me. *(Linda hums a soft lullaby.)* When that
team came out – he was the tallest, remember?

LINDA: Oh, yes. And in gold.

*(Biff enters the darkened kitchen, takes a cigarette, and leaves
20 the house. He comes downstage into a golden pool of light. He
smokes, staring at the night.)*

WILLY: Like a young god. Hercules – something like that. And
the sun, the sun all around him. Remember how he waved
to me? Right up from the field, with the representatives of
25 three colleges standing by? And the buyers I brought, and
the cheers when he came out – Loman, Loman, Loman! God
Almighty, he'll be great yet. A star like that, magnificent, can
never really fade away!

*(The light on Willy is fading. The gas heater begins to glow
30 through the kitchen wall, near the stairs, a blue flame beneath
red coils.)*

LINDA *(timidly)*: Willy dear, what has he got against you?

---

2 **to undersell oneself** [ˌ– –ˈ–] to ask for less than one is worth – 14 **Ebbets Field** name
of a football and baseball stadium in Brooklyn (demolished in 1960) – 14 **championship**
competiton to find the best team or player – 16 **to hum** to sing with one's lips closed –
16 **lullaby** [ˈlʌləbaɪ] a song to help children fall asleep – 18 **in gold** wearing a gold col-
ored helmet – 20 **in a golden pool of light** surrounded by a golden light – 22 **Hercules**
[ˈhɜːkjʊliːz] an ancient Greek hero known for his strength – 28 **to fade away** to slowly
disappear – 31 **coils** a set of metal rings connected together (Spirale) – 32 **timidly**
fearfully, cautiously

WILLY: I'm so tired. Don't talk any more. *(Biff slowly returns to the kitchen. He stops, stares toward the heater.)*
LINDA: Will you ask Howard to let you work in New York?
WILLY: First thing in the morning. Everything 'll be all right.

5   *(Biff reaches behind the heater and draws out a length of rubber tubing. He is horrified and turns his head toward Willy's room, still dimly lit, from which the strains of Linda's desperate but monotonous humming rise.)*

WILLY *(staring through the window into the moonlight)*: Gee,
10   look at the moon moving between the buildings!

   (Biff wraps the tubing around his hand and quickly goes up the stairs.)

---

6 **tubing** pipe – 6 **horrified** shocked, frightened – 7 **strains** sound – 8 **humming** sound made when one sings a melody with the lips closed – 8 **to rise** to increase – 11 **to wrap around** to wind [waɪnd] or twist around

Act Two

*Music is heard, gay and bright. The curtain rises as the music
fades away. Willy, in shirt sleeves, is sitting at the kitchen table,
sipping coffee, his hat in his lap. Linda is filling his cup when
she can.*

5 WILLY: Wonderful coffee. Meal in itself.

LINDA: Can I make you some eggs?

WILLY: No. Take a breath.

LINDA: You look so rested, dear.

WILLY: I slept like a dead one. First time in months. Imagine,
10   sleeping till ten on a Tuesday morning. Boys left nice and
   early, heh?

LINDA: They were out of here by eight o'clock.

WILLY: Good work!

LINDA: It was so thrilling to see them leaving together. I can't get
15   over the shaving lotion in this house!

WILLY *(Smiling)*: Mmm …

LINDA: Biff was very changed this morning. His whole attitude
   seemed to be hopeful. He couldn't wait to get downtown to
   see Oliver.

20 WILLY: He's heading for a change. There's no question, there
   simply are certain men that take longer to get – solidified.
   How did he dress?

LINDA: His blue suit. He's so handsome in that suit. He could be
   a – anything in that suit!

25 *(Willy gets up from the table. Linda holds his jacket for him.)*

WILLY: There's no question, no question at all. Gee, on the way
   home tonight I'd like to buy some seeds.

LINDA *(laughing)*: That'd be wonderful. But not enough sun gets
   back there. Nothing 'll grow any more.

---

2 **in shirt sleeves** wearing a shirt but no jacket – 2 **to sip** to drink in small quantities –
5 **meal in itself** like a complete meal – 7 **take a breath** [breθ] relax for a moment –
14 **thrilling** exciting, wonderful – 15 **shaving lotion** a kind of perfume put on the face
after shaving – 20 **to be heading for a change** to be about to change – 21 **solidified**
[–'– – –] established, settled, successful

WILLY: You wait, kid, before it's all over we're gonna get a little place out in the country, and I'll raise some vegetables, a couple of chickens …

LINDA: You'll do it yet, dear.

5   *(Willy walks out of his jacket. Linda follows him.)*

WILLY: And they'll get married, and come for a weekend. I'd build a little guest house. 'Cause I got so many fine tools, all I'd need would be a little lumber and some peace of mind.

LINDA *(joyfully)*: I sewed the lining …

10   WILLY: I could build two guest houses, so they'd both come. Did he decide how much he's going to ask Oliver for?

LINDA *(getting him into the jacket)*: He didn't mention it, but I imagine ten or fifteen thousand. You going to talk to Howard today?

15   WILLY: Yeah. I'll put it to him straight and simple. He'll just have to take me off the road.

LINDA: And Willy, don't forget to ask for a little advance, because we've got the insurance premium. It's the grace period now.

WILLY: That's a hundred …?

20   LINDA: A hundred and eight, sixty-eight. Because we're a little short again.

WILLY: Why are we short?

LINDA: Well, you had the motor job on the car …

WILLY: That goddam Studebaker!

25   LINDA: And you got one more payment on the refrigerator …

WILLY: But it just broke again!

LINDA: Well, it's old, dear.

WILLY: I told you we should've bought a well-advertised machine. Charley bought a General Electric and it's twenty

30   years old and it's still good, that son-of-a-bitch.

LINDA: But, Willy …

WILLY: Whoever heard of a Hastings refrigerator? Once in my life I would like to own something outright before it's broken!

---

1 **kid** informal way of addressing sb, usually a young person – 5 **Willy walks out of his jacket.** Willy walks away from the jacket his wife is holding without putting it on. – 15 **I'll put it to him straight and simple.** I'll say it to him directly and in plain words. – 16 **to take sb off the road** to give sb a job in an office after he was employed as a traveling salesman – 17 **advance** payment of salary before the time it is due (Vorschuss) – 18 **insurance premium** the sum of money paid regularly to an insurance company – 18 **grace period** extra time given before payment must be made – 23 **motor job** repair on the motor – 25 **one more payment** the last of a series of payments when buying sth on the installment plan – 30 **son-of-a-bitch** *(sl.)* sb one dislikes very much – 33 **outright** completely

I'm always in a race with the junkyard! I just finished paying for the car and it's on its last legs. The refrigerator consumes belts like a goddam maniac. They time those things. They time them so when you finally paid for them, they're used up.

5 LINDA *(buttoning up his jacket as he unbuttons it)*: All told, about two hundred dollars would carry us, dear. But that includes the last payment on the mortgage. After this payment, Willy, the house belongs to us.

WILLY: It's twenty-five years!

10 LINDA: Biff was nine years old when we bought it.

WILLY: Well, that's a great thing. To weather a twenty-five year mortgage is …

LINDA: It's an accomplishment.

WILLY: All the cement, the lumber, the reconstruction I put in
15 this house! There ain't a crack to be found in it any more.

LINDA: Well, it served its purpose.

WILLY: What purpose? Some stranger'll come along, move in, and that's that. If only Biff would take this house, and raise a family … *(He starts to go.)* Good-by, I'm late.

20 LINDA *(suddenly remembering)*: Oh, I forgot! You're supposed to meet them for dinner.

WILLY: Me?

LINDA: At Frank's Chop House on Forty-eighth near Sixth Avenue.

25 WILLY: Is that so! How about you?

LINDA: No, just the three of you. They're gonna blow you to a big meal!

WILLY: Don't say! Who thought of that?

LINDA: Biff came to me this morning, Willy, and he said, "Tell
30 Dad, we want to blow him to a big meal." Be there six o'clock. You and your two boys are going to have dinner.

WILLY: Gee whiz! That's really somethin'. I'm gonna knock Howard for a loop, kid. I'll get an advance, and I'll come home with a New York job. Goddammit, now I'm gonna do it!

---

1 **junkyard** place where useless and unwanted objects are taken to – 2 **on its last legs** about to break down, in very bad condition – 2 **to consume** to use up – 3 **maniac** ['meɪniæk] crazy person – 3 **to time** *here:* to build sth to last a certain time – 4 **used up** worn out, no longer useable – 5 **all told** altogether – 6 **to carry** to be enough for – 7 **mortgage** ['mɔːgɪdʒ] money borrowed from the bank to pay for a house – 11 **to weather** to survive a difficult period – 23 **Frank's Chop House** name of a restaurant – 23 **chop house** a medium-priced restaurant specializing in steaks and pork chops – 23 **Forty-eighth** Forty-eighth Street in midtown Manhattan – 26 **to blow sb to sth** *(sl.)* to pay for sb, to treat sb to sth – 32 **gee whiz** an expression of surprise – 32 **to knock sb for a loop** to impress sb very much

LINDA: Oh, that's the spirit, Willy!

WILLY: I will never get behind a wheel the rest of my life!

LINDA: It's changing. Willy, I can feel it changing!

WILLY: Beyond a question. G'by, I'm late. *(He starts to go*
5 *again.)*

LINDA *(calling after him as she runs to the kitchen table for a
handkerchief)*: You got your glasses?

WILLY: *(feels for them, then comes back in)*: Yeah, yeah, got my
glasses.

10 LINDA: *(giving him the handkerchief)*: And a handkerchief …

WILLY: Yeah, handkerchief.

LINDA: And your saccharine?

WILLY: Yeah, my saccharine.

LINDA: Be careful on the subway stairs.

15 *(She kisses him, and a silk stocking is seen hanging from her
hand. Willy notices it.)*

WILLY: Will you stop mending stockings? At least while I'm in
the house. It gets me nervous. I can't tell you. Please.

*(Linda hides the stocking in her hand as she follows Willy
20 across the forestage in front of the house.)*

LINDA: Remember, Frank's Chop House.

WILLY *(passing the apron)*: Maybe beets would grow out there.

LINDA *(laughing)*: But you tried so many times.

WILLY: Yeah. Well, don't work hard today. *(He disappears around
25 the right corner of the house.)*

LINDA: Be careful!

*(As Willy vanishes, Linda waves to him. Suddenly the phone
rings. She runs across the stage and into the kitchen and lifts
it.)*

30 LINDA: Hello? Oh, Biff! I'm so glad you called, I just … Yes, sure,
I just told him. Yes, he'll be there for dinner at six o'clock, I
didn't forget. Listen, I was just dying to tell you. You know
that little rubber pipe I told you about? That he connected
to the gas heater? I finally decided to go down the cellar this
35 morning and take it away and destroy it. But it's gone! Imagine? He took it away himself, it isn't there! *(She listens.)* When?

1 **that's the spirit** that's the right attidude – 2 **wheel** steering wheel – 4 **beyond a
question** there is no doubt – 4 **G'by** good-by – 12 **saccharine** [ˈsɔːkəriːn] an artificial
sweetener – 20 **forestage** see glossary – 22 **apron** the part of the stage in front of the
curtain – 22 **beet** rote Rübe – 32 **to be dying to do sth** to want very much to do sth

Oh, then you took it. Oh – nothing, it's just that I'd hoped he'd taken it away himself. Oh, I'm not worried, darling, because this morning he left in such high spirits, it was like the old days! I'm not afraid any more. Did Mr. Oliver see you? … Well,
5 you wait there then. And make a nice impression on him, darling. Just don't perspire too much before you see him. And have a nice time with Dad. He may have big news too! … That's right, a New York job. And be sweet to him tonight, dear. Be loving to him. Because he's only a little boat look-
10 ing for a harbor. *(She is trembling with sorrow and joy.)* Oh, that's wonderful, Biff, you'll save his life. Thanks, darling. Just put your arm around him when he comes into the restaurant. Give him a smile. That's the boy … Good-by, dear … You got your comb? … That's fine. Good-by, Biff dear.

15 *(In the middle of her speech, Howard Wagner, thirty-six, wheels on a small typewriter table on which is a wire-recording machine and proceeds to plug it in. This is on the left forestage. Light slowly fades on Linda as it rises on Howard. Howard is intent on threading the machine and only glances over his*
20 *shoulder as Willy appears.)*

WILLY: Pst! Pst!
HOWARD: Hello, Willy, come in.
WILLY: Like to have a little talk with you, Howard.
HOWARD: Sorry to keep you waiting. I'll be with you in a min-
25 ute.
WILLY: What's that, Howard?
HOWARD: Didn't you ever see one of these? Wire recorder.
WILLY: Oh. Can we talk a minute?
HOWARD: Records things. Just got delivery yesterday. Been driv-
30 ing me crazy, the most terrific machine I ever saw in my life. I was up all night with it.
WILLY: What do you do with it?
HOWARD: I bought it for dictation, but you can do anything with it. Listen to this. I had it home last night. Listen to what
35 I picked up. The first one is my daughter. Get this. *(He flicks*

---

3 **in high spirits** in a cheerful mood – 6 **to perspire** to sweat [swet] – 10 **sorrow** sadness – 15 **to wheel on** to push sth on wheels onto a stage, etc. – 16 **wire-recording machine** machine used before the tape recorder was introduced, for recording sounds – 17 **to proceed to do sth** to go on to do sth immediately after completing a previous action – 17 **to plug in** to connect to an electric current – 19 **to be intent on doing sth** to do sth with a great deal of concentration – 19 **to thread** [θred] to put sth, very thin through a small opening – 29 **to get delivery of sth** to receive sth at one's house or office – 35 **to flick** to move with a light quick blow

the switch and "Roll out the Barrel" is heard being whistled.)
Listen to that kid whistle.

WILLY: That is lifelike, isn't it?

HOWARD: Seven years old. Get that tone.

5 WILLY: Ts, ts. Like to ask a little favor if you …

(The whistling breaks off, and the voice of Howard's daughter is heard.)

HIS DAUGHTER: "Now you, Daddy."

HOWARD: She's crazy for me! *(Again the same song is whistled.)*
10 That's me! Ha! *(He winks).*

WILLY: You're very good! *(The whistling breaks off again. The machine runs silent for a moment.)*

HOWARD: Sh! Get this now, this is my son.

HIS SON: "The capital of Alabama is Montgomery; the capital of
15 Arizona is Phoenix; the capital of Arkansas is Little Rock; the capital of California is Sacramento …" *(and on, and on.)*

HOWARD *(holding up five fingers)*: Five years old, Willy!

WILLY: He'll make an announcer some day!

HIS SON *(continuing)*: "The capital …"

20 HOWARD: Get that – alphabetical order! *(The machine breaks off suddenly.)* Wait a minute. The maid kicked the plug out.

WILLY: It certainly is a …

HOWARD: Sh, for God's sake!

HIS SON: "It's nine o'clock, Bulova watch time. So I have to go to
25 sleep."

WILLY: That really is …

HOWARD: Wait a minute! The next is my wife.

(They wait).

HOWARD'S VOICE: "Go on, say something." *(Pause.)* "Well, you
30 gonna talk?"

HIS WIFE: "I can't think of anything."

HOWARD'S VOICE: "Well, talk – it's turning."

HIS WIFE *(shyly, beaten)*: "Hello." *(Silence.)* "Oh, Howard, I can't talk into this …"

35 HOWARD *(snapping the machine off)*: That was my wife.

1 **"Roll out the Barrel"** well-known lively drinking song – 4 **get that tone** listen to that sound – 9 **to be crazy for sb** to love sb very much – 10 **to wink** to close and open one eye quickly as a signal – 13 **get this now** listen to this now – 15 **Phoenix** ['fiːnɪks] **Arkansas** ['ɑːkənsɔː] – 18 **to make** to become – 21 **maid** woman hired to do the housework – 21 **plug** Stecker – 24 **Bulova** ['buːləvə] name of an American watch manufacturer – 24 **"Bulova watch time"** an advertising slogan – 33 **beaten** defeated – 35 **to snap off** to shut off with a quick movement

WILLY: That is a wonderful machine. Can we …

HOWARD: I tell you, Willy, I'm gonna take my camera, and my bandsaw, and all my hobbies, and out they go. This is the most fascinating relaxation I ever found.

5 WILLY: I think I'll get one myself.

HOWARD: Sure, they're only a hundred and a half. You can't do without it. Supposing you wanna hear Jack Benny, see? But you can't be at home at that hour. So you tell the maid to turn the radio on when Jack Benny comes on, and this automati-

10 cally goes on with the radio …

WILLY: And when you come home you …

HOWARD: You can come home twelve o'clock, one o'clock, any time you like, and you get yourself a Coke and sit yourself down, throw the switch, and there's Jack Benny's program in

15 the middle of the night!

WILLY: I'm definitely going to get one. Because lots of times I'm on the road, and I think to myself, what I must be missing on the radio!

HOWARD: Don't you have a radio in the car?

20 WILLY: Well, yeah, but who ever thinks of turning it on?

HOWARD: Say, aren't you supposed to be in Boston?

WILLY: That's what I want to talk to you about, Howard. You got a minute?

(He draws a chair in from the wing).

25 HOWARD: What happened? What're you doing here?

WILLY: Well …

HOWARD: You didn't crack up again, did you?

WILLY: Oh, no. No …

HOWARD: Geez, you had me worried there for a minute. What's

30 the trouble?

WILLY: Well, tell you the truth, Howard. I've come to the decision that I'd rather not travel any more.

HOWARD: Not travel! Well, what'll you do?

WILLY: Remember, Christmas time, when you had the party

35 here? You said you'd try to think of some spot for me here in town.

HOWARD: With us?

---

3 **bandsaw** Bandsäge – 7 **Jack Benny** TV and radio comedian (1894 - 1974) – 14 **to throw the switch** to turn a machine on or off – 24 **to draw in** to bring in – 24 **wing** side of stage not visible to the audience – 27 **to crack up** to have a serious accident with a car – 29 **geez** [dʒiːz] gee whiz, an exclamation of surprise or admiration – 35 **spot** job

WILLY: Well, sure.

HOWARD: Oh, yeah, yeah. I remember. Well, I couldn't think of anything for you, Willy.

WILLY: I tell ya, Howard. The kids are all grown up, y'know. I
5   don't need much any more. If I could take home – well, sixty-five dollars a week, I could swing it.

HOWARD: Yeah, but Willy, see I …

WILLY: I tell ya why. Howard. Speaking frankly and between the two of us, y'know – I'm just a little tired.

10 HOWARD: Oh, I could understand that, Willy. But you're a road man, Willy, and we do a road business. We've only got a half-dozen salesmen on the floor here.

WILLY: God knows, Howard. I never asked a favor of any man. But I was with the firm when your father used to carry you in
15 here in his arms.

HOWARD: I know that, Willy, but …

WILLY: Your father came to me the day you were born and asked me what I thought of the name of Howard, may he rest in peace.

20 HOWARD: I appreciate that, Willy, but there just is no spot here for you. If I had a spot I'd slam you right in, but I just don't have a single solitary spot.

(*He looks for his lighter. Willy has picked it up and gives it to him. Pause.*)

25 WILLY *(with increasing anger)*: Howard, all I need to set my table is fifty dollars a week.

HOWARD: But where am I going to put you, kid?

WILLY: Look, it isn't a question of whether I can sell merchandise, is it?

30 HOWARD: No, but it's a business, kid, and everybody's gotta pull his own weight.

WILLY *(desperately)*: Just let me tell you a story. Howard …

HOWARD: 'Cause you gotta admit, business is business.

WILLY *(angrily)*: Business is definitely business, but just listen
35 for a minute. You don't understand this. When I was a boy – eighteen, nineteen – I was already on the road. And there was a question in my mind as to whether selling had a future

---

6 **to swing** *(sl.)* to manage – 8 **frankly** openly – 10 **road man** traveling salesman –
11 **road business** business that does most of its business through traveling salesmen – 21 **I'd slam you right in** I'd immediately give you the job – 22 **solitary** another
word for "single", used for emphasis – 25 **to set my table** *here:* to earn enough to live
on – 28 **merchandise** goods – 30 **to pull one's own weight** to do one's job or share

for me. Because in those days I had a yearning to go to Alaska.
See, there were three gold strikes in one month in Alaska, and
I felt like going out. Just for the ride, you might say.

HOWARD *(barely interested)*: Don't say.

5 WILLY: Oh, yeah, my father lived many years in Alaska. He
was an adventurous man. We've got quite a little streak of
self-reliance in our family. I thought I'd go out with my older
brother and try to locate him, and maybe settle in the North
with the old man. And I was almost decided to go, when I met
10 a salesman in the Parker House. His name was Dave Single-
man. And he was eighty-four years old, and he'd drummed
merchandise in thirty-one states. And old Dave, he'd go up
to his room, y'understand, put on his green velvet slippers
– I'll never forget – and pick up his phone and call the buyers,
15 and without ever leaving his room, at the age of eighty-four,
he made his living. And when I saw that, I realized that selling was the greatest career a man could want. 'Cause what
could be more satisfying than to be able to go, at the age of
eighty-four, into twenty or thirty different cities, and pick up a
20 phone, and be remembered and loved and helped by so many
different people? Do you know? when he died – and by the
way he died the death of a salesman, in his green velvet slippers in the smoker of the New York, New Haven and Hartford,
going into Boston – when he died, hundreds of salesmen and
25 buyers were at his funeral. Things were sad on a lotta trains
for months after that. *(He stands up. Howard has not looked at
him.)* In those days there was personality in it, Howard. There
was respect, and comradeship, and gratitude in it. Today, it's
all cut and dried, and there's no chance for bringing friend-
30 ship to bear – or personality. You see what I mean? They don't
know me any more.

HOWARD *(moving away, to the right)*: That's just the thing, Willy.

WILLY: If I had forty dollars a week – that's all I'd need. Forty
dollars, Howard.

---

1 **a yearning** ['jɜːnɪŋ] a longing, a strong desire – 2 **strike** sudden valuable discovery –
3 **just for the ride** without any serious intention, just to have a look – 4 **Don't say** .
You don't say. = Is that right? – 6 **streak** tendency, quality in one's character – 7 **self-
reliance** ability to do things without the help of others – 8 **to locate** to find – 10 **Parker
House** a famous hotel in Boston – 11 **to drum** to sell – 13 **velvet** ['velvɪt] soft cloth
(Samt) – 23 **smoker** a railroad car in which smoking is permitted – 23 **New York, New
Haven and Hartford** a private railroad line – 25 **lotta** *(sl.)* lot of – 28 **gratitude**
['grætɪtjuːd] feeling of gratefulness – 29 **cut and dried** done quickly and without any
emotions – 29 **to bring sth to bear** to develop into sth useful

HOWARD: Kid, I can't take blood from a stone, I …

WILLY *(desperation is on him now)*: Howard, the year Al Smith was nominated, your father came to me and …

HOWARD *(starting to go* off*)*: I've got to see some people, kid.

5 WILLY *(stopping him)*. I'm talking about your father! There were promises made across this desk! You mustn't tell me you've got people to see – I put thirty-four years into this firm, Howard, and now I can't pay my insurance! You can't eat the orange and throw the peel away – a man is not a piece of fruit!

10 *(After a pause.)* Now pay attention. Your father – in 1928 I had a big year. I averaged a hundred and seventy dollars a week in commissions.

HOWARD *(impatiently)*: Now, Willy, you never averaged …

WILLY *(banging his hand on the desk)*: I averaged a hundred and

15 seventy dollars a week in the year of 1928! And your father came to me – or rather, I was in the office here – it was right over this desk – and he put his hand on my shoulder …

HOWARD *(getting up)*: You'll have to excuse me, Willy, I gotta see some people. Pull yourself together. *(Going out.)* I'll be back

20 in a little while.

(On Howard's exit, the light on his chair grows very bright and strange.)

WILLY: Pull myself together! What the hell did I say to him? My God, I was yelling at him! How could I? *(Willy breaks off, star-*

25 *ing at the light, which occupies the chair, animating it. He approaches this chair, standing across the desk from it.)* Frank, Frank, don't you remember what you told me that time? How you put your hand on my shoulder, and Frank… *(He leans on the desk and as he speaks the dead man's name he accidentally*

30 *switches on the recorder, and instantly)*

HOWARD'S SON: "… of New York is Albany. The capital of Ohio is Cincinnati, the capital of Rhode Island is …" *(The recitation continues.)*

WILLY *(leaping away with fright, shouting)*: Ha, Howard! How-

35 ard! Howard!

HOWARD *(rushing in)*: What happened?

---

1 **to take blood from a stone** to do an impossible task – 2 **desperation is on him** he is desperate – 2 **Al Smith** (1873 - 1944) unsuccessful Democratic candidate in the 1928 presidential election – 9 **peel** skin of an orange, banana etc. – 11 **to average** [ˈɔvrɪdʒ] *here:* to earn on the average (= im Durchschnitt) – 14 **to bang** to hit hard and with a loud noise – 19 **to pull oneself together** to get control of oneself – 25 **to animate** to make sth appear to be alive – 32 **recitation** [ˌresɪˈteɪʃn] the act of saying aloud material which has been learned by heart – 34 **to leap away** to jump away

WILLY *(pointing at the machine, which continues nasally, child-ishly, with the capital cities)*: Shut it off! Shut it off!

HOWARD *(pulling the plug out)*: Look, Willy …

WILLY *(pressing his hands to his eyes)*: I gotta get myself some
5   coffee. I'll get some coffee …

(Willy starts to walk out. Howard stops him.)

HOWARD *(rolling up the cord)*: Willy, look …

WILLY: I'll go to Boston.

HOWARD: Willy, you can't go to Boston for us.

10   WILLY: Why can't I go?

HOWARD: I don't want you to represent us. I've been meaning to
tell you for a long time now.

WILLY: Howard, are you firing me?

HOWARD: I think you need a good long rest, Willy.

15   WILLY: Howard …

HOWARD: And when you feel better, come back, and we'll see if
we can work something out.

WILLY: But I gotta earn money, Howard. I'm in no position
to …

20   HOWARD: Where are your sons? Why don't your sons give you a
hand?

WILLY: They're working on a very big deal.

HOWARD: This is no time for false pride, Willy. You go to your
sons and you tell them that you're tired. You've got two great

25   boys, haven't you?

WILLY: Oh, no question, no question, but in the meantime …

HOWARD: Then that's that, heh?

WILLY: All right, I'll go to Boston tomorrow.

HOWARD: No, no.

30   WILLY: I can't throw myself on my sons. I'm not a cripple!

HOWARD: Look, kid, I'm busy this morning.

WILLY *(grasping Howard's arm)*: Howard, you've got to let me
go to Boston!

HOWARD *(hard, keeping himself under control)*: I've got a line of
35   people to see this morning. Sit down, take five minutes, and
pull yourself together, and then go home, will ya? I need the
office, Willy. *(He starts to go, turns, remembering the recorder,*

---

1 **nasally** ['neɪzli] sounding as though produced through the nose – 7 **cord** Kabel – 17 **to
work sth out** to find a solution to a problem – 22 **a very big deal** an important business agreement – 30 **to throw yourself on sb** to make yourself dependent on sb, to
be a burden on sb – 30 **cripple** sb who has physical or mental problems and therefore
cannot move or think properly – 34 **a line of people** *here:* a lot of people

starts to push off the table holding the recorder.) Oh, yeah. Whenever you can this week, stop by and drop off the samples. You'll feel better, Willy, and then come back and we'll talk. Pull yourself together, kid, there's people outside.

5   *(Howard exits, pushing the table off left. Willy stares into space, exhausted. Now the music is heard – Ben's music – first distantly, then closer, closer. As Willy speaks, Ben enters from the right. He carries valise and umbrella.)*

WILLY: Oh, Ben, how did you do it? What is the answer? Did you
10   wind up the Alaska deal already?

BEN: Doesn't take much time if you know what you're doing. Just a short business trip. Boarding ship in an hour. Wanted to say good-by.

WILLY: Ben, I've got to talk to you.
15 BEN *(glancing at his watch)*: Haven't the time, William.

WILLY *(crossing the apron to Ben)*: Ben, nothing's working out. I don't know what to do.

BEN: Now, look here, William. I've bought timberland in Alaska and I need a man to look after things for me.
20 WILLY: God, timberland! Me and my boys in those grand outdoors?

BEN: You've a new continent at your doorstep, William. Get out of these cities, they're full of talk and time payments and courts of law. Screw on your fists and you can fight for a for-
25   tune up there.

WILLY: Yes, yes! Linda, Linda!

(Linda enters as of old, with the wash.)

LINDA: Oh, you're back?

BEN: I haven't much time.
30 WILLY: No, wait! Linda, he's got a proposition for me in Alaska.

LINDA: But you've got … *(To Ben.)* He's got a beautiful job here.

WILLY: But in Alaska, kid, I could …

LINDA: You're doing well enough, Willy!

BEN *(to Linda)*: Enough for what, my dear?
35 LINDA *(frightened of Ben and angry at him)*: Don't say those things to him! Enough to be happy right here, right now. *(To*

---

10 **to wind up** [waɪnd] to bring to an end, to settle – 10 **deal** business agreement or arrangement – 20 **timberland** area of forest used commercially – 20 **grand outdoors** great open countryside – 23 **time payments** small monthly payments made instead of paying the full cost of sth immediately – 24 **Screw on your fists …** Get aggressive like a boxer … – 30 **proposition** an interesting business arrangement

Willy, while Ben laughs.) Why must everybody conquer the world? You're well liked, and the boys love you, and someday – *(To Ben)* – why, old man Wagner told him just the other day that if he keeps it up he'll be a member of the firm, didn't he,

5   Willy?

WILLY: Sure, sure. I am building something with this firm, Ben, and if a man is building something he must be on the right track, mustn't he?

BEN: What are you building? Lay your hand on it. Where is it?

10 WILLY *(hesitantly)*: That's true, Linda, there's nothing.

LINDA: Why? *(To Ben.)* There's a man eighty-four years old –

WILLY: That's right, Ben, that's right. When I look at that man I say, what is there to worry about?

BEN: Bah!

15 WILLY: It's true, Ben. All he has to do is go into any city, pick up the phone, and he's making his living and you know why?

BEN *(picking up his valise)*: I've got to go.

WILLY *(holding Ben back)*: Look at this boy!

(Biff, in his high school sweater, enters carrying suitcase.
20 *Happy carries Biff's shoulder guards, gold helmet, and football*
pants.)

WILLY: Without a penny to his name, three great universities are begging for him, and from there the sky's the limit, because it's not what you do, Ben. It's who you know and the smile
25 on your face! It's contacts, Ben, contacts! The whole wealth of Alaska passes over the lunch table at the Commodore Hotel, and that's the wonder, the wonder of this country, that a man can end with diamonds here on the basis of being liked! *(He turns to Biff.)* And that's why when you get out on that field
30 today it's important. Because thousands of people will be rooting for you and loving you. *(To Ben, who has again begun to leave,)* And Ben! When he walks into a business office his name will sound out like a bell and all the doors will open to him! I've seen it, Ben, I've seen it a thousand times! You can't
35 feel it with your hand like timber, but it's there!

BEN: Good-by, William.

---

4 **to keep sth up** to continue to do sth in the same way – 6 **to build sth** *here:* to be on the way to success – 7 **to be on the right track** to be doing the right thing – 14 **Bah!** Nonsense! – 20 **shoulder guards** protection for the shoulders – 22 **without a penny to his name** without any money – 23 **to beg for sb** to want to have sb very much – 23 **the sky's the limit** there is no limit to the possibilities the future may bring – 31 **to root** to cheer, to support

WILLY: Ben, am I right? Don't you think I'm right? I value your advice.

BEN: There's a new continent at your doorstep, William. You could walk out rich. Rich! *(He is gone.)*

5 WILLY: We'll do it here, Ben! You hear me? We're gonna do it here!

(Young Bernard rushes in. The gay music of the Boys is heard.)

BERNARD: Oh, gee, I was afraid you left already!

WILLY: Why? What time is it?

10 BERNARD: It's half-past one!

WILLY: Well, come on, everybody! Ebbets Field next stop! Where's the pennants? *(He rushes through the wall-line of the kitchen and out into the living room.)*

LINDA *(to Biff)*: Did you pack fresh underwear?

15 BIFF *(who has been limbering tip)*: I want to go!

BERNARD: Biff, I'm carrying your helmet, ain't I?

HAPPY: No, I'm carrying the helmet.

BERNARD: Oh, Biff, you promised me.

HAPPY: I'm carrying the helmet.

20 BERNARD: How am I going to get in the locker room?

LINDA: Let him carry the shoulder guards. *(She puts her coat and hat on in the kitchen.)*

BERNARD: Can I, Biff? 'Cause I told everybody I'm going to be in the locker room.

25 HAPPY: In Ebbets Field it's the clubhouse.

BERNARD: I meant the clubhouse. Biff!

HAPPY: Biff!

BIFF *(grandly, after a slight pause)*: Let him carry the shoulder guards.

30 HAPPY *(as he gives Bernard the shoulder guards)*: Stay close to us now.

(Willy rushes in with the pennants.)

WILLY *(handing them out)*: Everybody wave when Biff comes out on the field. *(Happy and Bernard run off.)* You set now,
35 boy?

---

11 **next stop** the next place we're going to – 12 **pennant** small flag in the shape of a triangle – 15 **to limber up** to do exercises to loosen up the muscles before taking part in sports – 20 **locker room** room where players change clothes – 26 **clubhouse** house where a (sports) club has its office and locker rooms – 28 **grandly** in an impressive, superior way – 34 **set** ready

(The music has died away.)

BIFF: Ready to go, Pop. Every muscle is ready.

WILLY *(at the edge of the apron)*: You realize what this means?

BIFF: That's right, Pop.

5 WILLY *(feeling Biff's muscles)*: You're comin' home this afternoon captain of the All-Scholastic Championship Team of the City of New York.

BIFF: I got it, Pop. And remember, pal, when I take off my helmet, that touchdown is for you.

10 WILLY: Let's go! *(He is starting out, with his arm around Biff, when Charley enters, as of old, in knickers.)* I got no room for you, Charley.

CHARLEY: Room? For what?

WILLY: In the car.

15 CHARLEY: You goin' for a ride? I wanted to shoot some casino.

WILLY *(furiously)*: Casino! *(Incredulously.)* Don't you realize what today is?

LINDA: Oh, he knows, Willy. He's just kidding you.

WILLY: That's nothing to kid about!

20 CHARLEY: No, Linda, what's goin on?

LINDA: He's playing in Ebbets Field.

CHARLEY: Baseball in this weather?

WILLY: Don't talk to him. Come on, come on! *(He is pushing them out.)*

25 CHARLEY: Wait a minute, didn't you hear the news?

WILLY: What?

CHARLEY: Don't you listen to the radio? Ebbets Field just blew up.

WILLY: You go to hell! *(Charley laughs. Pushing them out.)* Come 30 on, come on! We're late.

CHARLEY *(as they go)*: Knock a homer, Biff, knock a homer!

WILLY *(the last to leave, turning to Charley)*: I don't think that was funny, Charley. This is the greatest day of his life.

CHARLEY: Willy, when are you going to grow up?

---

6 **All-Scholastic Championship Team** team that has won the most games played between public high schools in New York City – 15 **to shoot** *here:* to play – 16 **incredulously** [––––] with disbelief – 18 **to kid** to tease – 31 **to knock a homer** to hit a home run in a baseball game and therefore score a point

WILLY: Yeah, heh? When this game is over, Charley, you'll be laughing out of the other side of your face. They'll be calling him another Red Grange. Twenty-five thousand a year.

CHARLEY *(kidding)*: Is that so?

5 WILLY: Yeah, that's so.

CHARLEY: Well, then, I'm sorry, Willy. But tell me something.

WILLY: What?

CHARLEY: Who is Red Grange?

WILLY: Put up your hands. Goddam you, put up your hands!

10 *(Charley, chuckling, shakes his head and walks away, around the left corner of the stage. Willy follows him. The music rises to a mocking frenzy.)*

WILLY: Who the hell do you think you are, better than everybody else? You don't know everything, you big, ignorant, stupid …

15 Put up your hands!

(Light rises, on the right side of the forestage, on a small table in the reception room of Charley's office. Traffic sounds are heard. Bernard, now mature, sits whistling to himself. A pair of tennis rackets and an overnight bag are on the floor beside him.)

20 WILLY *(offstage)*: What are you walking away for? Don't walk away! If you're going to say something say it to my face! I know you laugh at me behind my back. You'll laugh out of the other side of your goddam face after this game. Touchdown! Touch-down! Eighty thousand people! Touchdown! Right between

25 the goal posts.

(Bernard is a quiet, earnest, but self-assured young man. Willy's voice is coming from right upstage now. Bernard lowers his feet off the table and listens. Jenny, his father's secretary, enters.)

JENNY *(distressed)*: Say, Bernard, will you go out in the hall?

30 BERNARD: What is that noise? Who is it?

JENNY: Mr. Loman. He just got off the elevator.

BERNARD *(getting up)*: Who's he arguing with?

JENNY: Nobody. There's nobody with him. I can't deal with him any more, and your father gets all upset everytime he comes.

---

2 **to laugh out of the other side of one's face** to regret having previously made fun of sth – 3 **Red Grange** Harold Grange (1903–1991) famous football player of the 1920's and '30's – 9 **Put up your hands.** Get ready to fight with me. – 12 **frenzy** great usually uncontrolled excitement – 26 **self-assured** self-confident – 27 **right upstage** at the back of the stage and on the right – 29 **distressed** upset, worried – 33 **I can't deal with him** I can't get along with him

I've got a lot of typing to do, and your father's waiting to sign
it. Will you see him?

WILLY *(entering)*: Touchdown! Touch – *(He sees Jenny.)* Jenny,
Jenny, good to see you. How're ya? Workin'? Or still honest?

5 JENNY: Fine. How've you been feeling?

WILLY: Not much any more, Jenny. Ha, ha! *(He is surprised to see
the rackets.)*

BERNARD: Hello, Uncle Willy.

WILLY *(almost shocked)*: Bernard! Well, look who's here! *(He
10 comes quickly, guiltily, to Bernard and warmly shakes his
hand.)*

BERNARD: How are you? Good to see you.

WILLY: What are you doing here?

BERNARD: Oh, just stopped by to see Pop. Get off my feet till my
15 train leaves. I'm going to Washington in a few minutes.

WILLY: Is he in?

BERNARD: Yes, he's in his office with the accountant. Sit down.

WILLY *(sitting down)*: What're you going to do in Washington?

BERNARD: Oh, just a case I've got there, Willy.

20 WILLY: That so? *(Indicating the rackets.)* You going to play tennis
there?

BERNARD: I'm staying with a friend who's got a court.

WILLY: Don't say. His own tennis court. Must be fine people, I
bet.

25 BERNARD: They are, very nice. Dad tells me Biff's in town.

WILLY *(with a big smile)*: Yeah, Biff's in. Working on a very big
deal, Bernard.

BERNARD: What's Biff doing?

WILLY: Well, he's been doing very big things in the West. But he
30 decided to establish himself here. Very big. We're having dinner. Did I hear your wife had a boy?

BERNARD: That's right. Our second.

WILLY: Two boys! What do you know!

BERNARD: What kind of a deal has Biff got?

35 WILLY: Well, Bill Oliver – very big sporting-goods man – he wants
Biff very badly. Called him in from the West. Long distance,

---

14 **to get off one's feet** to sit down, to rest one's feet – 17 **accountant** [–'– –] person
who inspects financial records and gives advice about how to pay the least taxes –
19 **case** an action brought before a court – 36 **long distance** a telephone call between
two cities a long way from each other

carte blanche, special deliveries. Your friends have their own private tennis court?

BERNARD: You still with the old firm, Willy?

WILLY *(after a pause)*: I'm – I'm overjoyed to see how you made
5   the grade, Bernard, overjoyed. It's an encouraging thing to see a young man really - really ... Looks very good for Biff – very ... *(He breaks off, then.)* Bernard ... *(He is so full of emotion, he breaks off again.)*

BERNARD: What is it, Willy?

10 WILLY *(small and alone)*: What – what's the secret?

BERNARD: What secret?

WILLY: How – how did you? Why didn't he ever catch on?

BERNARD: I wouldn't know that, Willy.

WILLY *(confidentially, desperately)*: You were his friend, his boy-
15   hood friend. There's something I don't understand about it. His life ended after that Ebbets Field game. From the age of seventeen nothing good ever happened to him.

BERNARD: He never trained himself for anything.

WILLY: But he did, he did. After high school he took so many
20   correspondence courses. Radio mechanics; television; God knows what, and never made the slightest mark.

BERNARD *(taking off his glasses)*: Willy, do you want to talk candidly?

WILLY *(rising, faces Bernard)*: I regard you as a very brilliant
25   man, Bernard. I value your advice.

BERNARD: Oh, the hell with the advice, Willy. I couldn't advise you. There's just one thing I've always wanted to ask you. When he was supposed to graduate, and the math teacher flunked him ...

30 WILLY: Oh, that son-of-a-bitch ruined his life.

BERNARD: Yeah, but, Willy, all he had to do was go to summer school and make up that subject.

WILLY: That's right, that's right.

BERNARD: Did you tell him not to go to summer school?

35 WILLY: Me? I begged him to go. I ordered him to go!

BERNARD: Then why wouldn't he go?

---

1 **carte blanche** [ˌkɑːt ˈblɑːnʃ] with no restrictions on expenses – 1 **special deliveries** letters sent at extra speed for an additional fee – 4 **to make the grade** to succeed, to reach a goal – 12 **to catch on** to understand, to learn how to do sth properly – 14 **confidentially** [kɒnfiˈdenʃli] said in secrecy – 21 **never made the slightest mark** never made any impression on him, never did him any good – 22 **candidly** openly and honestly – 24 **brilliant** intelligent – 25 **to value** to regard highly, to consider to be of great worth – 32 **to make up a subject** to retake a subject in which one has failed – 35 **to beg sb to do sth** to ask urgently

WILLY: Why? Why! Bernard, that question has been trailing me
like a ghost for the last fifteen years. He flunked the subject,
and laid down and died like a hammer hit him!

BERNARD: Take it easy, kid.

5　WILLY: Let me talk to you – I got nobody to talk to. Bernard, Bernard, was it my fault? Y'see? It keeps going around in my mind,
maybe I did something to him. I got nothing to give him.

BERNARD: Don't take it so hard.

WILLY: Why did he lay down? What is the story there? You were
10　his friend!

BERNARD: Willy, I remember, it was June, and our grades came
out. And he'd flunked math.

WILLY: That son-of-a-bitch!

BERNARD: No, it wasn't right then. Biff just got very angry, I
15　remember, and he was ready to enroll in summer school.

WILLY *(surprised)*: He was?

BERNARD: He wasn't beaten by it at all. But then, Willy, he disap-
peared from the block for almost a month. And I got the idea
that he'd gone up to New England to see you. Did he have a
20　talk with you then?

(Willy stares in silence.)

BERNARD: Willy?

WILLY *(with a strong edge of resentment in his voice)*: Yeah, he
came to Boston. What about it?

25　BERNARD: Well, just that when he came back – I'll never forget
this, it always mystifies me. Because I'd thought so well of Biff,
even though he'd always taken advantage of me. I loved him,
Willy, y'know? And he came back after that month and took
his sneakers – remember those sneakers with "University of
30　Virginia" printed on them? He was so proud of those, wore
them every day. And he took them down in the cellar, and
burned them up in the furnace. We had a fist fight. It lasted
at least half an hour. Just the two of us, punching each other
down the cellar and crying right through it. I've often thought
35　of how strange it was that I knew he'd given up his life. What
happened in Boston, Willy?

---

1 **to trail** to follow – 11 **grade** mark – 15 **to enroll** [–'–] to apply to take part in a course
etc. – 18 **block** neighborhood – 23 **edge** quality – 26 **to mystify** ['mɪstɪfaɪ] to puzzle –
27 **to take advantage of sb** to use sb for one's own good (jdn ausnutzen) – 32 **fist** the
hand closed tightly (Faust) – 33 **to punch sb** to hit sb with one's fist

(Willy looks at him as at an intruder.)

BERNARD: I just bring it up because you asked me.

WILLY *(angrily)*: Nothing. What do you mean, "What happened?" What's that got to do with anything?

5 BERNARD: Well, don't get sore.

WILLY: What are you trying to do, blame it on me? If a boy lays down is that my fault?

BERNARD: Now, Willy, don't get …

WILLY: Well, don't – don't talk to me that way! What does that
10 mean, "What happened?"

(Charley enters. He is in his vest, and he carries a bottle of bourbon.)

CHARLEY: Hey; you're going to miss that train. *(He waves the bottle.)*

15 BERNARD: Yeah, I'm going. *(He takes the bottle.)* Thanks, Pop. *(He picks up his rackets and bag.)* Good-by, Willy, and don't worry about it. You know, "If at first you don't succeed . . ."

WILLY: Yes, I believe in that.

BERNARD: But sometimes, Willy, it's better for a man just to walk
20 away.

WILLY: Walk away?

BERNARD: That's right.

WILLY: But if you can't walk away?

BERNARD *(after a slight pause)*: I guess that's when it's tough.
25 *(Extending his hand.)* Good-by, Willy.

WILLY *(shaking Bernard's hand)*: Good-by, boy.

CHARLEY *(an arm on Bernard's shoulder)*: How do you like this kid? Gonna argue a case in front of the Supreme Court.

BERNARD *(protesting)*: Pop!

30 WILLY *(genuinely shocked, pained, and happy)*: No! The Supreme Court!

BERNARD: I gotta run. 'By, Dad!

CHARLEY: Knock 'em dead, Bernard!

(Bernard goes off.)

---

1 **intruder** [–ʹ– –] uninvited person often with bad intentions – 5 **sore** angry – 6 **to lay down** to refuse to go on – 11 **vest** a piece of clothing for the top half of the body without arms often worn with a suit – 11 **bourbon** [ˈbɜːbən] an American whiskey – 17 "**If at first you don't succeed** …" "If at first you don't succeed, Try, try again." (proverb attributed to British educational writer William Edward Hickson, 1803 - 1870) – 24 **tough** [tʌf] especially difficult – 25 **to extend** to stretch or hold out – 28 **to argue a case** to give reasons before a court supporting a particular point of view – 28 **the Supreme Court** the highest court in the United States – 30 **pained** hurt

WILLY *(as Charley takes out his wallet)*: The Supreme Court! And
he didn't even mention it!

CHARLEY *(counting out money on the desk)*: He don't have to
– he's gonna do it.

5 WILLY: And you never told him what to do, did you? You never
took any interest in him.

CHARLEY: My salvation is that I never took any interest in anything. There's some money – fifty dollars. I got an accountant
inside.

10 WILLY: Charley, look … *(With difficulty.)* I got my insurance to
pay. If you can manage it – I need a hundred and ten dollars.

(Charley doesn't reply for a moment; merely stops moving.)

WILLY: I'd draw it from my bank but Linda would know, and
I …

15 CHARLEY: Sit down, Willy.

WILLY *(moving toward the chair)*: I'm keeping an account of
everything, remember. I'll pay every penny back. *(He sits.)*

CHARLEY: Now listen to me, Willy.

WILLY: I want you to know I appreciate …

20 CHARLEY *(sitting down on the table)*: Willy, what're you doin'?
What the hell is going on in your head?

WILLY: Why? I'm simply …

CHARLEY: I offered you a job. You make fifty dollars a week, and
I won't send you on the road.

25 WILLY: I've got a job.

CHARLEY: Without pay? What kind of a job is a job without pay?
(He rises.) Now, look, kid, enough is enough. I'm no genius
but I know when I'm being insulted.

WILLY: Insulted!

30 CHARLEY: Why don't you want to work for me?

WILLY: What's the matter with you? I've got a job.

CHARLEY: Then what're you walkin' in here every week for?

WILLY *(getting up)*: Well, if you don't want me to walk in here …

CHARLEY: I'm offering you a job.

35 WILLY: I don't want your goddam job!

CHARLEY: When the hell are you going to grow up?

---

1 **wallet** small flat case usually of leather to put paper money in – 7 **salvation** sth
that saves a person – 13 **to draw** to take money from a bank account – 16 **to keep an
account of sth** to keep a written record so that one can later remember things that
have happened, money that has been spent etc.

WILLY *(furiously)*: You big ignoramus, if you say that to me again I'll rap you one! I don't care how big you are! *(He's ready to fight.)*

(Pause.)

5 CHARLEY *(kindly, going to him)*: How much do you need, Willy?

WILLY: Charley, I'm strapped. I'm strapped. I don't know what to do. I was just fired.

CHARLEY: Howard fired you?

WILLY: That snotnose. Imagine that? I named him. I named him
10 Howard.

CHARLEY: Willy, when're you gonna realize that them things don't mean anything? You named him Howard, but you can't sell that. The only thing you got in this world is what you can sell. And the funny thing is that you're a salesman, and you
15 don't know that.

WILLY: I've always tried to think otherwise, I guess. I always felt that if a man was impressive, and well liked, that nothing …

CHARLEY: Why must everybody like you? Who liked J. P. Morgan? Was he impressive? In a Turkish bath he'd look like a butcher.
20 But with his pockets on he was very well liked. Now listen, Willy, I know you don't like me, and nobody can say I'm in love with you, but I'll give you a job because – just for the hell of it, put it that way. Now what do you say?

WILLY: I – I just can't work for you, Charley.

25 CHARLEY: What're you, jealous of me?

WILLY: I can't work for you, that's all, don't ask me why.

CHARLEY *(angered, takes out more* bills): You been jealous of me all your life, you damned fool! Here, pay your insurance. *(He puts the money in Willy's hand.)*

30 WILLY: I'm keeping strict accounts.

CHARLEY: I've got some work to do. Take care of yourself. And pay your insurance.

WILLY *(moving to the right)*: Funny, y'know? After all the high-ways, and the trains, and the appointments, and the years,
35 you end up worth more dead than alive.

---

2 **I'll rap you one** *(sl.)* I'll hit you so you won't forget it. – 2 **to rap** to hit –
6 **to be strapped** to be without any money – 9 **snotnose** *(sl.)* unpleasant, arrogant
young person – 11 **them things** *(sl.)* those things – 18 **J. P. Morgan** an important
banker(1837 - 1913) – 19 **Turkish bath** sauna – 30 **strict** *here:* very careful –
34 **appointment** [–'– –] an arrangement to meet sb at a certain time and place

CHARLEY: Willy, nobody's worth nothin' dead. *(After a slight pause.)* Did you hear what I said?

(Willy stands still, dreaming.)

CHARLEY: Willy!

5 WILLY: Apologize to Bernard for me when you see him. I didn't mean to argue with him. He's a fine boy. They're all fine boys, and they'll end up big – all of them. Someday they'll all play tennis together. Wish me luck, Charley. He saw Bill Oliver today.

10 CHARLEY: Good luck.

WILLY *(on the verge of tears)*: Charley, you're the only friend I got. Isn't that a remarkable thing? *(He goes out.)*

CHARLEY: Jesus!

(Charley stares after him a moment and follows. All light blacks
15 *out. Suddenly raucous music is heard, and a red glow rises*
behind the screen at right. Stanley, a young waiter, appears, car-
rying a table, followed by Happy, who is carrying two chairs.)

STANLEY *(putting the table down)*: That's all right, Mr. Loman, I can handle it myself. *(He turns and takes the chairs from*
20 *Happy and places them at the table.)*

HAPPY *(glancing around)*: Oh, this is better.

STANLEY: Sure, in the front there you're in the middle of all kinds of noise. Whenever you got a party, Mr. Loman, you just tell me and I'll put you back here. Y'know, there's a lotta people
25 they don't like it private, because when they go out they like to see a lotta action around them because they're sick and tired to stay in the house by theirself, But I know you, you ain't from Hackensack. You know what I mean?

HAPPY *(sitting down)*: So how's it coming, Stanley?

30 STANLEY: Ah, it's a dog's life. I only wish during the war they'd a took me in the Army. I coulda been dead by now.

HAPPY: My brother's back, Stanley.

STANLEY: Oh, he come back, heh? From the Far West.

HAPPY: Yeah, big cattle man, my brother, so treat him right. And
35 my father's coming too.

---

1 **nobody's worth nothin'** *(sl.)* nobody is worth anything – 11 **on the verge of** near, close to – 15 **raucous** ['rɔːkəs] rough and noisy – 19 **to handle sth** to take care of sth – 23 **a party** a group of people – 26 **tired to stay** *(sl.)* tired of staying – 27 **by theirself** *(sl.)* by themselves – 28 **Hackensack** ['- – -] unattractive city in New Jersey where most New Yorkers think hopelessly primitive types and losers live – 29 **how's it coming?** *(sl.)* how have you been doing? – 30 **the war** World War Two – 30 **they'd a took** *(sl.)* they would have taken

STANLEY: Oh, your father too!

HAPPY: You got a couple of nice lobsters?

STANLEY: Hundred per cent, big.

HAPPY: I want them with the claws.

5 STANLEY: Don't worry, I don't give you no mice. *(Happy laughs.)* How about some wine? It'll put a head on the meal.

HAPPY: No. You remember, Stanley, that recipe I brought you from overseas? With the champagne in it?

STANLEY: Oh, yeah, sure. I still got it tacked up yet in the kitchen.

10 But that'll have to cost a buck apiece anyways.

HAPPY: That's all right.

STANLEY: What'd you, hit a number or somethin'?

HAPPY: No, it's a little celebration. My brother is – I think he pulled off a big deal today. I think we're going into business

15 together.

STANLEY: Great! That's the best for you. Because a family business, you know what I mean – that's the best.

HAPPY: That's what I think.

STANLEY: 'Cause what's the difference? Somebody steals? It's

20 in the family. Know what I mean? *(Sotto voce).* Like this bartender here. The boss is goin' crazy what kinda leak he's got in the cash register. You put it in but it don't come out.

HAPPY *(raising his head)*: Sh!

STANLEY: What?

25 HAPPY: You notice I wasn't lookin' right or left, was I?

STANLEY: No.

HAPPY: And my eyes are closed.

STANLEY: So what's the …?

HAPPY: Strudel's comin'.

30 STANLEY *(catching on, looks around)*: Ah, no, there's no …

(He breaks off as a furred, lavishly dressed girl enters and sits at the next table. Both follow her with their eyes.)

---

2 **lobster** Hummer – 2 **hya** Hello. How are you? – 4 **claw** the "hand" of a lobster –
5 **I don't give you no mice** I won't give you any bad food – 6 **a head** *here:* an addition
that will make the meal a success – 7 **recipe** ['resəpi] Rezept – 9 **to tack up** to hang up
with small nails – 9 **yet** *(sl.)* still – 10 **a buck** *(sl.)* a dollar – 10 **apiece** for each person –
10 **anyways** *(sl.)* anyway – 12 **to hit a number** to win a game of chance – 14 **to pull
sth off** to be successful in doing sth very difficult – 20 **sotto voce** [ˌsɒtəʊ ˈvəʊtʃi] very
quietly and secretively – 20 **bartender** a person who serves people drinks at a bar –
21 **goin' crazy what kinda leak** going crazy about what kind of leak – 21 **leak** hole or
crack which allows sth to escape – 22 **cash register** Registrierkasse – 29 **strudel** *(sl.)*
good-looking woman – 30 **to catch on** to understand – 31 **furred** wearing a fur coat –
31 **lavishly** ['– – –] extravagantly, luxuriously

STANLEY: Geez, how'd ya know?

HAPPY: I got radar or something. *(Staring directly at her profile.)* Oooooooo … Stanley.

STANLEY: I think that's for you, Mr. Loman.

5 HAPPY: Look at that mouth. Oh, God. And the binoculars.

STANLEY: Geez, you got a life, Mr. Loman.

HAPPY: Wait on her.

STANLEY *(going to the Girl's table)*: Would you like a menu, ma'am?

10 GIRL: I'm expecting someone, but I'd like a …

HAPPY: Why don't you bring her – excuse me, miss, do you mind? I sell champagne, and I'd like you to try my brand. Bring her a champagne, Stanley.

GIRL: That's awfully nice of you.

15 HAPPY: Don't mention it. It's all company money. *(He laughs.)*

GIRL: That's a charming product to be selling, isn't it?

HAPPY: Oh, gets to be like everything else. Selling is selling, y'know.

GIRL: I suppose.

20 HAPPY: You don't happen to sell, do you?

GIRL: No, I don't sell.

HAPPY: Would you object to a compliment from a stranger? You ought to be on a magazine cover.

GIRL *(looking at him a little archly)*: I have been.

25 *(Stanley comes in with a glass of champagne.)*

HAPPY: What'd I say before, Stanley? You see? She's a cover girl.

STANLEY: Oh, I could see, I could see.

HAPPY *(to the Girl)*: What magazine?

GIRL: Oh, a lot of them. *(She takes the drink.)* Thank you.

30 HAPPY: You know what they say in France, don't you? "Champagne is the drink of the complexion" – Hya, Biff!

(Biff has entered and sits with Happy.)

BIFF: Hello, kid. Sorry I'm late.

HAPPY: I just got here. Uh, Miss …?

---

1 **geez** [dʒiːz] gee whiz, an exclamation of surprise or admiration – 1 **how'd ya know** *(sl,)* how did you know – 2 **radar** [ˈreɪdɑː] *here:* the ability to know sth is there without actually seeing it – 5 **binoculars** [–'– – –] *here:* breasts – 12 **brand** product from a particular firm – 24 **archly** cleverly, playfully – 26 **cover girl** a woman who has appeared on the cover of a magazine – 31 **the drink of the complexion** the kind of drink that will keep your face looking young and healthy

GIRL: Forsythe.

HAPPY: Miss Forsythe, this is my brother.

BIFF: Is Dad here?

HAPPY: His name is Biff. You might've heard of him. Great foot-
5   ball player.

GIRL: Really? What team?

HAPPY: Are you familiar with football?

GIRL: No, I'm afraid I'm not.

HAPPY: Biff is quarterback with the New York Giants.

10 GIRL: Well, that is nice, isn't it? *(She drinks.)*

HAPPY: Good health.

GIRL: I'm happy to meet you.

HAPPY: That's my name. Hap. It's really Harold, but at West Point
    they called me Happy.

15 GIRL *(now really impressed)*: Oh, I see. How do you do? *(She
    turns her profile.)*

BIFF: Isn't Dad coming?

HAPPY: You want her?

BIFF: Oh, I could never make that.

20 HAPPY: I remember the time that idea would never come into
    your head. Where's the old confidence, Biff?

BIFF: I just saw Oliver …

HAPPY: Wait a minute. I've got to see that old confidence again.
    Do you want her? She's on call.

25 BIFF: Oh, no. *(He turns to look at the Girl.)*

HAPPY: I'm telling you. Watch this. *(Turning to the Girl.)* Honey?
    (She turns to him). Are you busy?

GIRL: Well, I am … but I could make a phone call.

HAPPY: Do that, will you, honey? And see if you can get a friend.
30   We'll be here for a while. Biff is one of the greatest football
    players in the country.

GIRL *(standing up)*: Well, I'm certainly happy to meet you.

HAPPY: Come back soon.

GIRL: I'll try.

35 HAPPY: Don't try, honey, try hard.

---

9 **quarterback** an important player on a football team – 9 **New York Giants** a professional football team – 13 **West Point** U.S. Military Academy on the Hudson River in New
York, which trains and educates the elite of the U.S. Army – 19 **I could never make that**
I would never be able to succeed with her – 24 **she's on call** she's available if you want
her – 29 **honey** darling, dear

(The Girl exits. Stanley follows, shaking his head in bewildered admiration.)

HAPPY: Isn't that a shame now? A beautiful girl like that? That's why I can't get married. There's not a good woman in a thou-
5   sand. New York is loaded with them, kid!

BIFF: Hap, look …

HAPPY: I told you she was on call!

BIFF *(strangely unnerved)*: Cut it out, will ya? I want to say some-thing to you.

10 HAPPY: Did you see Oliver?

BIFF: I saw him all right. Now look, I want to tell Dad a couple of things and I want you to help me.

HAPPY: What? Is he going to back you?

BIFF: Are you crazy? You're out of your goddam head, you know
15   that?

HAPPY: Why? What happened?

BIFF *(breathlessly)*: I did a terrible thing today, Hap. It's been the strangest day I ever went through. I'm all numb, I swear.

HAPPY: You mean he wouldn't see you?

20 BIFF: Well, I waited six hours for him, see? All day. Kept sending my name in. Even tried to date his secretary so she'd get me to him, but no soap.

HAPPY: Because you're not showin' the old confidence, Biff. He remembered you, didn't he?

25 BIFF *(stopping Happy with a gesture)*: Finally, about five o'clock, he comes out. Didn't remember who I was or anything. I felt like such an idiot, Hap.

HAPPY: Did you tell him my Florida idea?

BIFF: He walked away. I saw him for one minute. I got so mad
30   I could've torn the walls down! How the hell did I ever get the idea I was a salesman there? I even believed myself that I'd been a salesman for him! And then he gave me one look and – I realized what a ridiculous lie my whole life has been! We've been talking in a dream for fifteen years. I was a ship-
35   ping clerk.

HAPPY: What'd you do?

---

1 **bewildered** [bɪˈwɪldəd] confused, unable to understand – 5 **loaded** full – 8 **unnerved** upset, having lost one's self-control – 8 **cut it out** stop it – 13 **to back** to support usually financially – 14 **to be out of one's head** to be insane, crazy – 18 **to be numb** [nʌm] to have lost all sense of feeling and emotion – 21 **to date sb** to arrange to go out with sb of the opposite sex – 22 **no soap** *(sl.)* it didn't work out

BIFF *(with great tension and wonder)*: Well, he left, see. And the
secretary went out. I was all alone in the waiting room. I don't
know what came over me, Hap. The next thing I know I'm
in his office – paneled walls, everything. I can't explain it. I
5   – Hap, I took his fountain pen.

HAPPY: Geez, did he catch you?

BIFF: I ran out. I ran down all eleven flights. I ran and ran and
ran.

HAPPY: That was an awful dumb – what'd you do that for?

10 BIFF *(agonized)*: I don't know, I just – wanted to take something,
I don't know. You gotta help me, Hap, I'm gonna tell Pop.

HAPPY: You crazy? What for?

BIFF: Hap, he's got to understand that I'm not the man somebody lends that kind of money to. He thinks I've been spiting

15 him all these years and it's eating him up.

HAPPY: That's just it. You tell him something nice.

BIFF: I can't.

HAPPY: Say you got a lunch date with Oliver tomorrow.

BIFF: So what do I do tomorrow?

20 HAPPY: You leave the house tomorrow and come back at night
and say Oliver is thinking it over. And he thinks it over for a
couple of weeks, and gradually it fades away and nobody's
the worse.

BIFF: But it'll go on forever!

25 HAPPY: Dad is never so happy as when he's looking forward to
something!

(Willy enters.)

HAPPY: Hello, scout!

WILLY: Gee, I haven't been here in years!

30   *(Stanley has followed Willy in and sets a chair for him. Stanley
starts off but Happy stops him.)*

HAPPY: Stanley!

(Stanley stands by, waiting for an order.)

2 I don't know what came over me I don't know what caused me to do what I did –
4 **paneled** [pɒnld] decorated with wooden boards – 5 **fountain pen** pen that must be
filled with ink – 7 **flight** flight of steps, set of steps between two levels – 9 **dumb** [dʌm]
here: stupid – 10 **agonized** mentally suffering – 14 **to spite sb** to do sth purposely to
upset or annoy sb, usually when one thinks one has previously been unfairly treated by
the other person – 15 **it's eating him up** it's sth that is constantly bothering him – 22 **to
fade** to disappear slowly – 22 **nobody's the worse** nobody is in a worse position than
before – 28 **scout** informal form of address for sb one likes – 30 **sets a chair for him**
places a chair at the table for him

BIFF *(going to Willy with guilt, as to an invalid)*: Sit down, Pop. You want a drink?

WILLY: Sure, I don't mind.

BIFF: Let's get a load on.

5 WILLY: You look worried.

BIFF: N-no. *(To Stanley.)* Scotch all around. Make it doubles.

STANLEY: Doubles, right. *(He goes.)*

WILLY: You had a couple already, didn't you?

BIFF: Just a couple, yeah.

10 WILLY: Well, what happened, boy? *(Nodding affirmatively, with a smile.)* Everything go all right?

BIFF *(takes a breath, then reaches out and grasps Willy's hand)*: Pal … *(He is smiling bravely, and Willy is smiling too.)* I had an experience today.

15 HAPPY: Terrific, Pop.

WILLY: That so? What happened?

BIFF *(high, slightly alcoholic, above the earth)*: I'm going to tell you everything from first to last. It's been a strange day. *(Silence. He looks around, composes himself as best he can,*

20 *but his breath keeps breaking the rhythm of his voice.)* I had to wait quite a while for him, and …

WILLY: Oliver?

BIFF: Yeah, Oliver. All day, as a matter of cold fact. And a lot of – instances – facts, Pop, facts about my life came back to me.

25 Who was it, Pop? Who ever said I was a salesman with Oliver?

WILLY: Well, you were.

BIFF: No, Dad, I was a shipping clerk.

WILLY: But you were practically …

30 BIFF *(with determination)*: Dad, I don't know who said it first, but I was never a salesman for Bill Oliver.

WILLY: What're you talking about?

BIFF: Let's hold on to the facts tonight, Pop. We're not going to get anywhere bullin' around. I was a shipping clerk.

35 WILLY *(angrily)*: All right, now listen to me …

---

1 **guilt** feeling of having done sth wrong – 1 **invalid** ['ɪnvəlɪd] a person who is so sick that he can't care for himself – 4 **to get a load on** *(sl.)* to get drunk – 6 **doubles** drinks with twice the normal amount of alcohol – 10 **to nod affirmatively** to move one's head up and down in an encouraging way – 17 **above the earth** not quite in the real world – 19 **to compose oneself** to get back one's self control – 23 **as a matter of cold fact** to tell the honest truth – 30 **with determination** firmly, intent on continuing – 33 **let's hold on to the facts** let's only talk about the facts – 34 **to bull around** to waste time talking about foolish things

BIFF: Why don't you let me finish?

WILLY: I'm not interested in stories about the past or any crap of that kind because the woods are burning, boys, you understand? There's a big blaze going on all around. I was fired today.

BIFF *(shocked)*: How could you be?

WILLY: I was fired, and I'm looking for a little good news to tell your mother, because the woman has waited and the woman has suffered. The gist of it is that I haven't got a story left in my head, Biff. So don't give me a lecture about facts and aspects. I am not interested. Now what've you got to say to me?

(Stanley enters with three drinks. They wait until he leaves.)

WILLY: Did you see Oliver?

BIFF: Jesus, Dad!

WILLY: You mean you didn't go up there?

HAPPY: Sure he went up there.

BIFF: I did. I – saw him. How could they fire you?

WILLY *(on the edge of his chair)*: What kind of a welcome did he give you?

BIFF: He won't even let you work on commission?

WILLY: I'm out! *(Driving.)* So tell me, he gave you a warm welcome?

HAPPY: Sure, Pop, sure!

BIFF *(driven)*: Well, it was kind of…

WILLY: I was wondering if he'd remember you. *(To Happy.)* Imagine, man doesn't see him for ten, twelve years and gives him that kind of a welcome!

HAPPY: Damn right!

BIFF *(trying to return to the offensive)*: Pop, look …

WILLY: You know why he remembered you, don't you? Because you impressed him in those days.

BIFF: Let's talk quietly and get this down to the facts, huh?

WILLY *(as though Biff had been interrupting)*: Well, what happened? It's great news, Biff. Did he take you into his office or'd you talk in the waiting room?

BIFF: Well, he came in, see, and …

---

2 **crap** *(vulgar)* nonsense – 4 **there's a big blaze going on all around** there's a major crisis – 4 **blaze** a destructive fire that spreads rapidly – 9 **gist** [dʒɪst] basic idea, essence – 10 **lecture** *here:* talk criticizing what sb has done – 21 **driving** trying to force an answer from sb – 32 **to get sth down to facts** to discuss the facts only

WILLY *(with a big smile)*: What'd he say? Betcha he threw his
  arm around you.

BIFF: Well, he kinda …

WILLY: He's a fine man. *(To Happy.)* Very hard man to see,
5 y'know.

HAPPY *(agreeing)*: Oh, I know.

WILLY *(to Biff)*: Is that where you had the drinks?

BIFF: Yeah, he gave me a couple of – no, no!

HAPPY *(cutting in)*: He told him my Florida idea.

10 WILLY: Don't interrupt. *(To Biff.)* How'd he react to the Florida
  idea?

BIFF: Dad, will you give me a minute to explain?

WILLY: I've been waiting for you to explain since I sat down here!
  What happened? He took you into his office and what?

15 BIFF: Well – I talked. And – and he listened, see.

WILLY: Famous for the way he listens, y'know. What was his
  answer?

BIFF: His answer was – *(He breaks off, suddenly angry.)* Dad,
  you're not letting me tell you what I want to tell you!

20 WILLY *(accusing, angered)*: You didn't see him, did you?

BIFF: I did see him!

WILLY: What'd you insult him or something? You insulted him,
  didn't you?

BIFF: Listen, will you let me out of it, will you just let me out of
25 it!

HAPPY: What the hell!

WILLY: Tell me what happened!

BIFF *(to Happy)*: I can't talk to him!

(A single trumpet note jars the ear. The light of green leaves
30 *stains the house, which holds the air of night and a dream.*
  Young Bernard enters and knocks on the door of the house.)

YOUNG BERNARD *(frantically)*: Mrs. Loman, Mrs. Loman!

HAPPY: Tell him what happened!

BIFF *(to Happy)*: Shut up and leave me alone!

35 WILLY: No, no! You had to go and flunk math!

BIFF: What math? What're you talking about?

---

1 **betcha** *(sl.)* I bet you = I'm sure – 4 **hard man to see** it's difficult to get a chance to
talk to him alone – 9 **to cut in** to interrupt – 20 **accusing** showing one thinks the other
person has done wrong – 22 **to insult** [–ʹ–] to say things to a person meant to hurt
him, to be rude to sb – 22 **What'd you insult him …** What? Did you insult him … –
24 **let me out of it** let me finish explaining – 29 **to jar** to irritate, to sound unpleasant –
30 **to stain** to color sth on the surface – 32 **frantically** wildly, in panic

YOUNG BERNARD: Mrs. Loman, Mrs. Loman!

(Linda appears in the house, as of old.)

WILLY *(wildly)*: Math, math, math!

BIFF: Take it easy, Pop!

5 YOUNG BERNARD: Mrs. Loman!

WILLY *(furiously)*: If you hadn't flunked you'd've been set by now!

BIFF: Now, look, I'm gonna tell you what happened, and you're going to listen to me.

10 YOUNG BERNARD: Mrs. Loman!

BIFF: I waited six hours …

HAPPY: What the hell are you saying?

BIFF: I kept sending in my name but he wouldn't see me. So finally he … *(He continues unheard as light fades low on the*

15 *restaurant.)*

YOUNG BERNARD: Biff flunked math!

LINDA: No!

YOUNG BERNARD: Birnbaum flunked him! They won't graduate him!

20 LINDA: But they have to. He's gotta go to the university. Where is he? Biff! Biff!

YOUNG BERNARD: No, he left. He went to Grand Central.

LINDA: Grand – You mean he went to Boston!

YOUNG BERNARDS: Is Uncle Willy in Boston?

25 LINDA: Oh, maybe Willy can talk to the teacher. Oh, the poor, poor boy!

(Light on house area snaps out.)

BIFF *(at the table, now audible, holding up a gold fountain pen)*: … so I'm washed up with Oliver, you understand? Are

30 you listening to me?

WILLY *(at a loss)*: Yeah, sure. If you hadn't flunked …

BIFF: Flunked what? What're you talking about?

WILLY: Don't blame everything on me! I didn't flunk math – you did! What pen?

35 HAPPY: That was awful dumb, Biff, a pen like that is worth …

WILLY *(seeing the pen for the first time)*: You took Oliver's pen?

---

6 **furiously** very angrily – 6 **you'd have been set** you would have had a successful life –
22 **Grand Central** one of the main train stations in New York City – 27 **to snap out** to
switch off quickly – 28 **audible** [ˈɔːdɪbl] able to be heard – 29 **I'm washed up with Oliver**
I won't get any help from Oliver any more – 31 **at a loss** not knowing what to do or say

Biff *(weakening)*: Dad, I just explained it to you.

Willy: You stole Bill Oliver's fountain pen!

Biff: I didn't exactly steal it! That's just what I've been explaining to you!

5 Happy: He had it in his hand and just then Oliver walked in, so he got nervous and stuck it in his pocket!

Willy: My God, Biff!

Biff: I never intended to do it, Dad!

Operator's voice: Standish Arms, good evening!

10 Willy *(shouting)*: I'm not in my room!

Biff *(frightened)*: Dad, what's the matter? *(He and Happy stand up.)*

Operator: Ringing Mr. Loman for you!

Willy: I'm not there, stop it!

15 Biff *(horrified, gets down on one knee before* Willy): Dad, I'll make good, I'll make good. *(Willy tries to get to his feet. Biff holds him down.)* Sit down now.

Willy: No, you're no good, you're no good for anything.

Biff: I am, Dad, I'll find something else, you understand? Now

20 don't worry about anything, *(He holds up Willy's face.)* Talk to me, Dad.

Operator: Mr. Loman does not answer. Shall I page him?

Willy *(attempting to stand, as though to rush and silence the Operator)*: No, no, no!

25 Happy: He'll strike something, Pop.

Willy: No, no …

Biff *(desperately, standing over* Willy): Pop, listen! Listen to me! I'm telling you something good. Oliver talked to his partner about the Florida idea. You listening? He – he talked to his

30 partner, and he came to me … I'm going to be all right, you hear? Dad, listen to me, he said it was just a question of the amount!

Willy: Then you … got it?

Happy: He's gonna be terrific, Pop!

35 Willy *(trying to stand)*: Then you got it, haven't you? You got it! You got it!

---

9 **operator** ['- - -] person who connects one telephone caller to another – 9 **Standish Arms** name of a hotel – 13 **Ringing Mr. Loman for you!** I'm trying to connect you with Mr. Loman. – 15 **horrified** filled with shock and fear – 16 **to make good** to do sth good to show one is sorry for what one has done in the past – 22 **to page sb** to call sb over a loudspeaker or by sending sb around who calls out that person's name – 23 **to rush** to move quickly – 23 **to silence sb** to make sb quiet – 25 **to strike sth** *here:* to be successful at sth

BIFF *(agonized, holds Willy down)*: No, no. Look, Pop. I'm supposed to have lunch with them tomorrow. I'm just telling you this so you'll know that I can still make an impression, Pop. And I'll make good somewhere, but I can't go tomorrow, see?

5 WILLY: Why not? You simply …

BIFF: But the pen, Pop!

WILLY: You give it to him and tell him it was an oversight!

HAPPY: Sure, have lunch tomorrow!

BIFF: I can't say that …

10 WILLY: You were doing a crossword puzzle and accidentally used his pen!

BIFF: Listen, kid, I took those balls years ago, now I walk in with his fountain pen? That clinches it, don't you see? I can't face him like that! I'll try elsewhere.

15 PAGE'S VOICE: Paging Mr. Loman!

WILLY: Don't you want to be anything?

BIFF: Pop, how can I go back?

WILLY: You don't want to be anything, is that what's behind it?

BIFF *(now angry at Willy for not crediting his sympathy)*: Don't
20 take it that way! You think it was easy walking into that office after what I'd done to him? A team of horses couldn't have dragged me back to Bill Oliver!

WILLY: Then why'd you go?

BIFF: Why did I go? Why did I go! Look at you! Look at what's
25 become of you!

(Off left, The Woman laughs.)

WILLY: Biff, you're going to go to that lunch tomorrow, or …

BIFF: I can't go. I've got no appointment!

HAPPY: Biff, for…!

30 WILLY: Are you spiting me?

BIFF: Don't take it that way! Goddammit!

WILLY *(strikes Biff and falters away from the table)*: You rotten little louse! Are you spiting me?

THE WOMAN: Someone's at the door, Willy!

35 BIFF: I'm no good, can't you see what I am?

HAPPY *(separating them)*: Hey, you're in a restaurant! Now cut it out, both of you! *(The girls enter.)* Hello, girls, sit down.

(The Woman laughs, off left.)

---

7 **oversight** ['– –] mistake – 13 **that clinches it** that settles everything – 15 **page** boy in a hotel who carries messages, calls people, etc. – 19 **to credit** to take seriously – 32 **to falter** to walk unsteadily

MISS FORSYTHE: I guess we might as well. This is Letta.

THE WOMAN: Willy, are you going to wake up?

BIFF *(ignoring* Willy): How're ya, miss, sit down. What do you drink?

5 MISS FORSYTHE: Letta might not be able to stay long.

LETTA: I gotta get up very early tomorrow. I got jury duty. I'm so excited! Were you fellows ever on a jury?

BIFF: No, but I been in front of them! *(The girls laugh.)* This is my father.

10 LETTA: Isn't he cute? Sit down with us, Pop.

HAPPY: Sit him down, Biff!

BIFF *(going to him)*: Come on, slugger, drink us under the table. To hell with it! Come on, sit down, pal.

(On Biff's last insistence, Willy is about to sit.)

15 THE WOMAN *(now urgently)*: Willy are you going to answer the door!

(The Woman's call pulls Willy back. He starts right, befuddled.)

BIFF: Hey, where are you going?

20 WILLY: Open the door.

BIFF: The door?

WILLY: The washroom … the door … where's the door?

BIFF *(leading Willy to the left)*: Just go straight down.

(Willy moves left.)

25 THE WOMAN: Willy, Willy, are you going to get up, get up, get up, get up?

(Willy exits left.)

LETTA: I think it's sweet you bring your daddy along.

MISS FORSYTHE: Oh, he isn't really your father!

30 BIFF *(at left, turning to her resentfully)*: Miss Forsythe, you've just seen a prince walk by. A fine, troubled prince. A hard-working,

---

1 **we might as well** there's nothing better to do – 6 **jury** group of citizens who are appointed to listen to a case in court and decide if an accused person is innocent or guilty – 6 **jury duty** duty to serve on a jury – 10 **cute** sweet, attractive – 10 **Pop** Dad, often considered an insult when not addressing one's own father – 12 **slugger** in baseball a player who hits the ball very hard;*here:* a person who can push all difficulties aside – 12 **to drink sb under the table** to be able to drink more alcohol than the other person – 14 **on Biff's last insistence** when Biff asks him to do it for the last time – 17 **befuddled** confused

unappreciated prince. A pal, you understand? A good companion. Always for his boys.

LETTA: That's so sweet.

HAPPY: Well, girls, what's the program? We're wasting time. Come
5   on, Biff. Gather round. Where would you like to go?

BIFF: Why don't you do something for him?

HAPPY: Me!

BIFF: Don't you give a damn for him, Hap?

HAPPY: What're you talking about? I'm the one who –

10 BIFF: I sense it, you don't give a good goddam about him. *(He
takes the rolled up hose from his pocket and puts it on the table
in front of Happy.)* Look what I found in the cellar, for Christ's
sake. How can you bear to let it go on?

HAPPY: Me? Who goes away? Who runs off and –

15 BIFF: Yeah, but he doesn't mean anything to you. You could help
him – I can't! Don't you understand what I'm talking about?
He's going to kill himself, don't you know that?

HAPPY: Don't I know it! Me!

BIFF: Hap, help him! Jesus … help him … Help me, help me, I
20   can't bear to look at his face! *(Ready to weep, he hurries out,
up right.)*

HAPPY *(starting after him)*: Where are you going?

MISS FORSYTHE: What's he so mad about?

HAPPY: Come on, girls, we'll catch up with him.

25 MISS FORSYTHE *(as Happy pushes her out)*: Say, I don't like that
temper of his!

HAPPY: He's just a little overstrung, he'll be all right!

WILLY *(off left, as The Woman laughs)*: Don't answer! Don't
answer!

30 LETTA: Don't you want to tell your father …

HAPPY: No, that's not my father. He's just a guy. Come on, we'll
catch Biff, and, honey, we're going to paint this town! Stanley,
where's the check! Hey, Stanley!

(They exit. Stanley looks toward left.)

35 STANLEY *(calling to Happy indignantly)*: Mr. Loman! Mr.
Loman!

---

1 **companion** a person to do things with – 5 **gather round** get closer together – 8 **Don't
you give a damn for him?** Don't you care for him even a little bit? – 11 **hose** rubber
pipe – 27 **overstrung** stressed, over sensitive – 32 **to paint this town** to paint the town
red, to celebrate wildly – 35 **indignantly** angrily because of sth unfair

(Stanley picks up a chair and follows them off. Knocking is heard off left. The Woman enters, laughing. Willy follows her. She is in a black slip; he is buttoning his shirt. Raw, sensuous music accompanies their speech.)

5   WILLY: Will you stop laughing? Will you stop?

THE WOMAN: Aren't you going to answer the door? He'll wake the whole hotel.

WILLY: I'm not expecting anybody.

THE WOMAN: Whyn't you have another drink, honey, and stop
10   being so damn self-centered?

WILLY: I'm so lonely.

THE WOMAN: You know you ruined me, Willy? From now on, whenever you come to the office, I'll see that you go right through to the buyers. No waiting at my desk anymore, Willy.
15   You ruined me.

WILLY: That's nice of you to say that.

THE WOMAN: Gee, you are self-centered! Why so sad? You are the saddest, self-centeredest soul I ever did see-saw. *(She laughs. He kisses her.)* Come on inside, drummer boy. It's silly to be
20   dressing in the middle of the night. *(As knocking is heard.)* Aren't you going to answer the door?

WILLY: They're knocking on the wrong door.

THE WOMAN: But I felt the knocking. And he heard us talking in here. Maybe the hotel's on fire!

25   WILLY *(his terror rising)*: It's a mistake.

THE WOMAN: Then tell him to go away!

WILLY: There's nobody there.

THE WOMAN: It's getting on my nerves, Willy. There's somebody standing out there and it's getting on my nerves!

30   WILLY *(pushing her away from him)*: All right, stay in the bathroom here, and don't come out. I think there's a law in Massachusetts about it, so don't come out. It may be that new room clerk. He looked very mean. So don't come out. It's a mistake, there's no fire.

---

3 **slip** piece of clothing worn under a dress (Unterrock) – 3 **raw** vulgar – 3 **sensuous** giving pleasure to the mind or body – 9 **whyn't** *(sl.)* why don't you – 18 **self-centeredest** *(sl.)* the most self-centered – 18 **see-saw** a play on the words: "see," meaning to meet, and "see-saw," which is a long board found in playgrounds that goes up and down when two people sit at the ends. The phrase also has a sexual meaning – 19 **drummer** traveling salesman – 31 **there's a law about it** *here:* there's a law forbidding unmarried couples to share the same room in a hotel – 32 **room clerk** the person in a hotel responsible for giving the guests their room – 33 **mean** likely to cause trouble, strict

(The knocking is heard again. He takes a few steps away from her, and she vanishes into the wing. The light follows him, and now he is facing Young Biff, who carries a suitcase. Biff steps toward him. The music is gone.)

5   BIFF: Why didn't you answer?

WILLY: Biff! What are you doing in Boston?

BIFF: Why didn't you answer? I've been knocking for five minutes, I called you on the phone …

WILLY: I just heard you. I was in the bathroom and had the door
10   shut. Did anything happen home?

BIFF: Dad – I let you down.

WILLY: What do you mean?

BIFF: Dad …

WILLY: Biffo, what's this about? *(Putting his arm around Biff.)*
15   Come on, let's go downstairs and get you a malted.

BIFF: Dad, I flunked math.

WILLY: Not for the term?

BIFF: The term. I haven't got enough credits to graduate.

WILLY: You mean to say Bernard wouldn't give you the
20   answers?

BIFF: He did, he tried, but I only got a sixty-one.

WILLY: And they wouldn't give you four points?

BIFF: Birnbaum refused absolutely. I begged him, Pop, but he won't give me those points. You gotta talk to him before they
25   close the school. Because if he saw the kind of man you are, and you just talked to him in your way, I'm sure he'd come through for me. The class came right before practice, see, and I didn't go enough. Would you talk to him? He'd like you, Pop. You know the way you could talk.

30   WILLY: You're on. We'll drive right back.

BIFF: Oh, Dad, good work! I'm sure he'll change it for you!

WILLY: Go downstairs and tell the clerk I'm checkin' out. Go right down.

---

11 **to let sb down** to disappoint sb – 15 **malted** malted milk, drink made with ice-cream, milk, and malt – 17 **term** division in a school year, there are usually two or three terms in a school year – 18 **credits** points achieved for each course taken – 21 **a sixty-one** sixty-one out of a possible hundred points. Below sixty-five would be considered a failing mark – 26 **to come through for sb** to give sb a chance – 27 **practice** training for sports – 28 **I didn't go enough** I didn't go to Birnbaum's class often enough – 30 **You're on.** I accept your challenge. – 32 **to check out** to give your key back and arrange to leave a hotel

BIFF: Yes, sir! See, the reason he hates me, Pop – one day he was late for class so I got up at the blackboard and imitated him. I crossed my eyes and talked with a lithp.

WILLY *(laughing)*: You did? The kids like it?

5 BIFF: They nearly died laughing!

WILLY: Yeah? What'd you do?

BIFF: The thquare root of thixthy-twee is … *(Willy bursts out laughing; Biff joins him.)* And in the middle of it he walked in!

10 *(Willy laughs and The Woman joins in offstage.)*

WILLY *(without hesitation)*: Hurry downstairs and …

BIFF: Somebody in there?

WILLY: No, that was next door.

(The Woman laughs offstage.)

15 BIFF: Somebody got in your bathroom!

WILLY: No, it's the next room, there's a party …

THE WOMAN *(enters, laughing; she lisps this)*: Can I come in? There's something in the bathtub, Willy, and it's moving!

(Willy looks at Biff, who is staring open-mouthed and horrified
20 *at The Woman.)*

WILLY: Ali – you better go back to your room. They must be finished painting by now. They're painting her room so I let her take a shower here. Go back, go back … *(He pushes her.)*

THE WOMAN *(resisting)*: But I've got to get dressed, Willy, I can't
25 –

WILLY: Get out of here! Go back, go back … *(Suddenly striving for the ordinary.)* This is Miss Francis, Biff, she's a buyer. They're painting her room. Go back, Miss Francis, go back …

THE WOMAN: But my clothes, I can't go out naked in the hall!

30 WILLY *(pushing her offstage)*: Get outa here! Go back, go back!

(Biff slowly sits down on his suitcase as the argument contin-
ues offstage.)

THE WOMAN: Where's my stockings? You promised me stockings, Willy!

---

3 **to cross your eyes** to look to the center with both eyes – 3 **lithp** lisp, a speech problem where an "s" is pronounced as "th" – 7 **thquare root of thixthy-twee** square root of sixty-three said by sb with a lisp – 18 **bathtub** object in which you take a bath – 26 **to strive for the ordinary** to try to return everything to normal when sth unpleasant happens

WILLY: I have no stockings here!

THE WOMAN: You had two boxes of size nine sheers for me, and I want them!

WILLY: Here, for God's sake, will you get outa here!

5 THE WOMAN *(enters holding a box of stockings)*: I just hope there's nobody in the hall. That's all I hope. *(To Biff.)* Are you football or baseball?

BIFF: Football.

THE WOMAN *(angry, humiliated)*: That's me too. G'night. *(She
10 snatches her clothes from Willy, and walks out.)*

WILLY *(after a pause)*: Well, better get going. I want to get to the school first thing in the morning. Get my suits out of the closet. I'll get my valise. *(Biff doesn't move.)* What's the matter! *(Biff remains motionless, tears falling.)* She's a buyer. Buys
15 for J. H. Simmons. She lives down the hall – they're painting. You don't imagine – *(He breaks off. After a pause.)* Now listen, pal, she's just a buyer. She sees merchandise in her room and they have to keep it looking just so … *(Pause. Assuming command.)* All right, get my suits. *(Biff doesn't move.)* Now stop
20 crying and do as I say. I gave you an order. Biff, I gave you an order! Is that what you do when I give you an order? How dare you cry! *(Putting his arm around Biff.)* Now look, Biff, when you grow up you'll understand about these things. You mustn't – you mustn't overemphasize a thing like this. I'll see
25 Birnbaum first thing in the morning.

BIFF: Never mind.

WILLY *(getting down beside Biff)*: Never mind! He's going to give you those points. I'll see to it.

BIFF: He wouldn't listen to you.

30 WILLY: He certainly will listen to me. You need those points for the U. of Virginia.

BIFF: I'm not going there.

WILLY: Heh? If I can't get him to change that mark you'll make it up in summer school. You've got all summer to –

35 BIFF *(his weeping breaking from him)*: Dad …

WILLY *(infected by it)*: Oh, my boy …

BIFF: Dad …

---

2 **sheers** stockings of very thin material – 9 **to humiliate sb** [hjuːˈmɪlieɪt] to cause sb to lose his/her pride – 10 **to snatch** to take sth quickly – 13 **closet** [ˈklɒzɪt] a small room for hanging clothes in – 18 **just so** in good condition – 18 **assuming command** taking control and giving orders – 35 **his weeping breaking from him** he cannot hold back his tears any more – 36 **to infect sb** to cause an identical reaction in sb

WILLY: She's nothing to me, Biff. I was lonely, I was terrible lonely.

BIFF: You – you gave her Mama's stockings! *(His tears break through and he rises to go.)*

5 WILLY *(grabbing for Biff)*: I gave you an order!

BIFF: Don't touch me, you – liar!

WILLY: Apologize for that!

BIFF: You fake! You phony little fake! You fake! *(Overcome, he turns quickly and weeping fully goes out with his suitcase.*

10 *Willy is left on the floor on his knees.)*

WILLY: I gave you an order! Biff, come back here or I'll beat you! Come back here! I'll whip you!

(Stanley comes quickly in from the right and stands in front of Willy.)

15 WILLY *(shouts at Stanley)*: I gave you an order …

STANLEY: Hey, let's pick it up, pick it up, Mr. Loman. *(He helps Willy to his feet.)* Your boys left with the chippies. They said they'll see you home.

(A second waiter watches some distance away.)

20 WILLY: But we were supposed to have dinner together.

(Music is heard, Willy's theme.)

STANLEY: Can you make it?

WILLY: I'll – sure, I can make it. *(Suddenly concerned about his clothes.)* Do I – I look all right?

25 STANLEY: Sure, you look all right. *(He flicks a speck off Willy's lapel.)*

WILLY: Here – here's a dollar.

STANLEY: Oh, your son paid me. It's all right.

WILLY *(putting it in Stanley's hand)*: No, take it. You're a good

30 boy.

STANLEY: Oh, no, you don't have to …

WILLY: Here – here's some more, I don't need it any more. *(After a slight pause.)* Tell me – is there a seed store in the neighborhood?

35 STANLEY: Seeds? You mean like to plant?

---

8 **fake** sb who is not what he claims to be – 8 **phony** [ˈfəʊni] false – 12 **to whip** to hit with a piece of leather or a stick – 16 **pick it up** hurry up – 17 **chippy** *(sl.)* prostitute – 18 **see you home** see you at home – 22 **Can you make it?** Can you manage? – 25 **to flick** to move sth away by hitting or pushing it sharply – 25 **speck** a very small piece of dirt – 26 **lapel** [ləˈpel] the part of a jacket folded back below the neck (Revers)

(As Willy turns, Stanley slips the money back into his jacket pocket.)

WILLY: Yes. Carrots, peas …

STANLEY: Well, there's hardware stores on Sixth Avenue, but it
5   may be too late now.

WILLY *(anxiously)*: Oh, I'd better hurry. I've got to get some
seeds. *(He starts off to the right.)* I've got to get some seeds,
right away. Nothing's planted. I don't have a thing in the
ground.

10   *(Willy hurries out as the light goes down. Stanley moves over to
the right after him, watches him o The other waiter has been
staring at Willy.)*

STANLEY *(to the waiter)*: Well, whatta you looking at?

*(The waiter picks up the chairs and moves off right. Stanley
15   takes the table and follows him. The light fades on this area.
There is a long pause, the sound of the flute coming over. The
light gradually rises on the kitchen, which is empty. Happy
appears at the door of the house, followed by Biff. Happy is
carrying a large bunch of long-stemmed roses. He enters the
20   kitchen, looks around for Linda. Not seeing her, he turns to Biff,
who is just outside the house door, and makes a gesture with
his hands, indicating "Not here, I guess." He looks into the living room and freezes. Inside, Linda, unseen is seated, Willy's
coat on her lap. She rises ominously and quietly and moves
25   toward Happy, who backs up into the kitchen, afraid.)*

HAPPY: Hey, what're you doing up? *(Linda says nothing but
moves toward him implacably.)* Where's Pop? *(He keeps backing to the right and now Linda is in full view in the doorway to
the living room.)* Is he sleeping?

30   LINDA: Where were you?

HAPPY *(trying to laugh it off)*: We met two girls, Mom, very fine
types. Here, we brought you some flowers. *(Offering them to
her.)* Put them in your room, Ma.

---

4 **hardware store** store where you can get tools and equipment for the house and garden – 13 **whatta** *(sl.)* what are – 19 **bunch** a number of things held together – 19 **long-
stemmed** with a long stem (Stiel) – 23 **to freeze** to suddenly stop moving and remain
totally still – 24 **ominously** ['ɒmɪnəsli] in a manner that indicates sth unpleasant is
going to happen – 25 **to back up** to step backwards – 26 **What're you doing up?** Why
aren't you in bed yet? – 27 **implacably** [ɪmˈplækəbli] with a strong feeling of anger that
will not go away quickly – 31 **to laugh off** to make a serious thing appear unimportant
or amusing

(She knocks them to the floor at Biff's feet. He has now come inside and closed the door behind him. She stares at Biff, silent.)

HAPPY: Now what'd you do that for? Mom, I want you to have
5   some flowers …

LINDA *(cutting Happy off, violently to Biff)*: Don't you care whether he lives or dies?

HAPPY *(going to the stairs)*: Come upstairs, Biff.

BIFF *(with a flare of disgust, to Happy)*: Go away from me! *(To*
10   *Linda.)* What do you mean, lives or dies? Nobody's dying around here, pal.

LINDA: Get out of my sight! Get out of here!

BIFF: I wanna see the boss.

LINDA: You're not going near him!

15   BIFF: Where is he? *(He moves into the living room and Linda follows.)*

LINDA *(shouting after Biff)*: You invite him for dinner. He looks forward to it all day – *(Biff appears in his parent's bedroom, looks around, and exits)* – and then you desert him there.
20   There's no stranger you'd do that to!

HAPPY: Why? He had a swell time with us. Listen, when I – *(Linda comes back into the kitchen)* – desert him I hope I don't outlive the day!

LINDA: Get out of here!

25   HAPPY: Now look, Mom …

LINDA: Did you have to go to women tonight? You and your lousy rotten whores!

(Biff re-enters the kitchen.)

HAPPY: Mom, all we did was follow Biff around trying to cheer
30   him up! *(To Biff.)* Boy, what a night you gave me!

LINDA: Get out of here, both of you, and don't come back! I don't want you tormenting him any more. Go on now, get your things together! *(To Biff.)* You can sleep in his apartment. *(She starts to pick up the flowers and stops herself.)* Pick up this
35   stuff, I'm not your maid any more. Pick it up, you bum, you!

---

9 flare *here:* a sudden outburst – **9 disgust** a strong feeling of dislike at sb's bad behavior – **19 to desert sb** [‑ˈ‑] to leave sb at the moment this person needs help – **21 swell** *(sl.)* fine, wonderful – **22 I hope I don't outlive the day!** I'd rather die than desert him – **27 rotten** morally corrupt – **27 whore** [ˈhɔː] prostitute – **32 to torment** [‑ˈ‑] to cause sb to suffer – **35 maid** woman hired to do the housework – **35 bum** worthless person, a good-for-nothing

(Happy turns his back to her in refusal. Biff slowly moves over and gets down on his knees, picking up the flowers.)

LINDA: You're a pair of animals! Not one, not another living soul would have had the cruelty to walk out on the man in a res-
5   taurant!

BIFF *(not looking at her)*: Is that what he said?

LINDA: He didn't have to say anything. He was so humiliated he nearly limped when he came in.

HAPPY: But, Mom, he had a great time with us …
10 BIFF *(cutting him off violently)*: Shut up!

(Without another word, Happy goes upstairs.)

LINDA: You! You didn't even go in to see if he was all right!

BIFF *(still on the floor in front of Linda, the flowers in his hand; with self-loathing)*: No. Didn't. Didn't do a damned thing. How
15 do you like that, heh? Left him babbling in a toilet.

LINDA: You louse. You …

BIFF: Now you hit it on the nose! *(He gets up, throws the flowers in the wastebasket.)* The scum of the earth, and you're looking at him!

20 LINDA: Get out of here!

BIFF: I gotta talk to the boss, Mom. Where is he?

LINDA: You're not going near him. Get out of this house!

BIFF *(with absolute assurance, determination)*: No. We're gonna have an abrupt conversation, him and me.

25 LINDA: You're not talking to him.

(Hammering is heard from outside the house, off right. Biff turns toward the noise.)

LINDA *(suddenly pleading)*: Will you please leave him alone?

BIFF: What's he doing out there?
30 LINDA: He's planting the garden!

BIFF *(quietly)*: Now? Oh, my God!

(Biff moves outside, Linda following. The light dies down on them and comes up on the center of the apron as Willy walks

---

4 **to walk out on sb** to leave sb suddenly especially when there is a disagreement –
8 **to limp** to walk with difficulty because one leg is hurt – 14 **self-loathing** [ˈləʊðɪŋ] feeling of disgust about oneself – 15 **to babble** to talk quickly in a confused way – 17 **you
hit it on the nose** you describe it absolutely correctly – 18 **scum** anything worthless,
trash – 23 **assurance** [əˈʃʊrəns] feeling of confidence and lack of doubt – 28 **to plead** to
ask in an emotional way

into it. He is carrying a flashlight, a hoe, and a handful of seed
packet. He raps the top of the hoe sharply to fix it firmly, and
then moves to the left, measuring off the distance with his foot.
He holds the flashlight to look at the seed packets, reading off
5   *the instructions. He is in the blue of night.)*

WILLY: Carrots … quarter-inch apart. Rows … one-foot rows.
(He measures it off.) One foot. *(He puts down a package and*
measures off.) Beets. *(He puts down another package and mea-*
sures again.) Lettuce. *(He reads the package, puts it down.)*
10   One foot – *(He breaks off as Ben appears at the right and*
moves slowly down to him.) What a proposition, ts, ts. Terrific,
terrific. 'Cause she's suffered, Ben, the woman has suffered.
You understand me? A man can't go out the way he came in,
Ben, a man has got to add up to something. You can't, you
15   can't – *(Ben moves toward him as though to interrupt.)* You
gotta consider, now. Don't answer so quick. Remember, it's a
guaranteed twenty-thousand-dollar proposition. Now look,
Ben, I want you to go through the ins and outs of this thing
with me. I've got nobody to talk to, Ben, and the woman has
20   suffered, you hear me?
BEN *(standing still, considering)*: What's the proposition?
WILLY: It's twenty thousand dollars on the barrelhead. Guaranteed, gilt-edged, you understand?
BEN: You don't want to make a fool of yourself. They might not
25   honor the policy.
WILLY: How can they dare refuse? Didn't I work like a coolie to
meet every premium on the nose? And now they don't pay
off? Impossible!
BEN: It's called a cowardly thing, William.
30   WILLY: Why? Does it take more guts to stand here the rest of my
life ringing up a zero?

---

1 **flashlight** [ˈ– –] portable electric lamp; torch*(B.E.)* – 1 **hoe** [həʊ] gardening tool
(Hacke) – 2 **to rap** to hit sth with a series of quick blows – 9 **lettuce** [ˈletɪs] Kopfsalat –
11 **what a proposition** what a good suggestion for a business deal – 14 **to add up**
to sth to be worth sth in the end – 18 **the ins and outs** all the details – 22 **on the**
barrelhead in cash – 23 **gilt-edged** of the highest value – 24 **they might not honor the**
policy they (the insurance company) may not pay the money due – 26 **coolie** [ˈkuːli] a
Chinese worker, i.e. sb who works hard for little money – 26 **to meet** to pay – 27 **on the**
nose on time – 30 **guts** *(coll.)* courage – 31 **to ring up a zero** to make no money, to be a
complete failure

BEN *(yielding)*: That's a point, William. *(He moves, thinking, turns.)* And twenty thousand – that is something one can feel with the hand, it is there.

WILLY *(now assured, with rising power)*: Oh, Ben, that's the whole
5 beauty of it! I see it like a diamond, shining in the dark, hard and rough, that I can pick up and touch in my hand. Not like – like an appointment! This would not be another damned-fool appointment, Ben, and it changes all the aspects. Because he thinks I'm nothing, see, and so he spites me. But the funeral
10 *(Straightening up.)* Ben, that funeral will be massive! They'll come from Maine, Massachusetts, Vermont, New Hampshire! All the oldtimers with the strange license plates – that boy will be thunderstruck, Ben, because he never realized – I am known! Rhode Island, New York, New Jersey – I am known,
15 Ben, and he'll see it with his eyes once and for all. He'll see what I am, Ben! He's in for a shock, that boy!

BEN *(coming down to the edge of the garden)*: He'll call you a coward.

WILLY *(suddenly fearful)*: No, that would be terrible.

20 BEN: Yes. And a damned fool.

WILLY: No, no, he mustn't, I won't have that! *(He is broken and desperate.)*

BEN: He'll hate you, William.

(The gay music of the Boys is heard.)

25 WILLY: Oh, Ben, how do we get back to all the great times? Used to be so full of light and comradeship, the sleigh-riding in winter and the ruddiness on his cheeks. And always some kind of good news coming up, always something nice coming up ahead. And never even let me carry the valises in the house,
30 and simonizing, simonizing that little red car! Why, why can't I give him something and not have him hate me?

BEN: Let me think about it. *(He glances at his watch.)* I still have a little time. Remarkable proposition, but you've got to be sure you're not making a fool of yourself.

35 *(Ben drifts off upstage and goes out of sight. Biff comes down from the left.)*

---

1 **yielding** letting himself be persuaded – 12 **license plate** sign on the back and front of a car with letters and numbers on it which identify the car – 13 **thunderstruck** very surprised – 16 **he's in for a shock** he is going to get a shock – 26 **sleigh** [sleɪ] vehicle that slides along on the snow – 27 **ruddiness** reddish healthy color

WILLY *(suddenly conscious of Biff, turns and looks up at him, then begins picking up the packages of seeds in confusion.)*: Where the hell is that seed? *(Indignantly.)* You can't see nothing out here! They boxed in the whole goddam neighborhood!

5 BIFF: There are people all around here. Don't you realize that?

WILLY: I'm busy. Don't bother me.

BIFF *(taking the hoe from* Willy): I'm saying good-by to you, Pop. *(Willy looks at him, silent, unable to move.)* I'm not coming back any more.

10 WILLY: You're not going to see Oliver tomorrow?

BIFF: I've got no appointment, Dad.

WILLY: He put his arm around you, and you've got no appointment?

BIFF: Pop, get this now, will you? Everytime I've left it's been a
15 fight that sent me out of here. Today I realized something about myself and I tried to explain it to you and I – I think I'm just not smart enough to make any sense out of it for you. To hell with whose fault it is or anything like that. *(He takes Willy's arm.)* Let's just wrap it up, heh? Come on in, we'll tell
20 Mom. *(He gently tries to pull Willy to left.)*

WILLY *(frozen, immobile, with guilt in his voice)*: No, I don't want to see her.

BIFF: Come on! *(He pulls again, and Willy tries to pull away.)*

WILLY *(highly nervous)*: No, no, I don't want to see her.

25 BIFF *(tries to look into Willy's face, as if to find the answer there)*: Why don't you want to see her?

WILLY *(more harshly now)*: Don't bother me, will you?

BIFF: What do you mean, you don't want to see her? You don't want them calling you yellow, do you? This isn't your fault; it's
30 me, I'm a bum. Now come inside! *(Willy strains to get away.)* Did you hear what I said to you?

(Willy pulls away and quickly goes by himself into the house. Biff follows.)

LINDA *(to* Willy): Did you plant, dear?

35 BIFF *(at the door, to Linda)*. All right, we had it out. I'm going and I'm not writing any more.

---

1 **conscious of** ['kɒnʃəs] aware of – 14 **get this** listen to this – 19 **to wrap sth up** to finish sth – 27 **harshly** coldly, showing no sympathy – 27 **to bother sb** to irritate sb, to annoy sb – 29 **yellow** *(coll.)* cowardly – 30 **to strain** to make a great effort to do sth – 35 **to have it out** to openly discuss a serious disagreement

LINDA *(going to Willy in the kitchen)*: I think that's the best way, dear. 'Cause there's no use drawing it out, you'll just never get along.

(Willy doesn't respond.)

5 BIFF: People ask where I am and what I'm doing, you don't know, and you don't care. That way it'll be off your mind and you can start brightening up again. All right? That clears it, doesn't it? *(Willy is silent, and Biff goes to him.)* You gonna wish me luck, scout? *(He extends his hand.)* What do you say?

10 LINDA: Shake his hand, Willy.

WILLY *(turning to her, seething with hurt)*: There's no necessity to mention the pen at all, y'know.

BIFF *(gently)*: I've got no appointment, Dad.

WILLY *(erupting fiercely)*. He put his arm around …?

15 BIFF: Dad, you're never going to see what I am, so what's the use of arguing? If I strike oil I'll send you a check. Meantime forget I'm alive.

WILLY *(to Linda)*: Spite, see?

BIFF: Shake hands, Dad.

20 WILLY: Not my hand.

BIFF: I was hoping not to go this way.

WILLY: Well, this is the way you're going. Good-by.

(Biff looks at him a moment, then turns sharply and goes to the stairs.)

25 WILLY *(stops him with)*: May you rot in hell if you leave this house!

BIFF *(turning)*: Exactly what is it that you want from me?

WILLY: I want you to know, on the train, in the mountains, in the valleys, wherever you go, that you cut down your life for

30 spite!

BIFF: No, no.

WILLY: Spite, spite, is the word of your undoing! And when you're down and out, remember what did it. When you're rot-

---

2 **to draw sth out** to let sth continue for longer than necessary – 4 **to respond** to answer – 7 **to brighten up** to become cheerful – 7 **that clears it** that settles everything, that gets rid of all the problems – 11 **to seethe** [siːð] to be very excited (from anger, indignation) – 14 **to erupt** to burst out, to suddenly get angry – 14 **fiercely** terribly, violently – 16 **to strike oil** to find oil, to become rich – 18 **spite** desire to hurt sb in return for sth bad that person has done to you – 25 **May you rot in hell.** I hope you'll be miserable forever. – 29 **you cut down your life** you ruined your life – 32 **undoing** [–ˈ– –] sth that causes one's ruin – 33 **down and out** with no friends, money or self-respect

ting somewhere beside the railroad tracks, remember, and don't you dare blame it on me!

BIFF: I'm not blaming it on you!

WILLY: I won't take the rap for this, you hear?

5   *(Happy comes down the stairs and stands on the bottom step, watching.)*

BIFF: That's just what I'm telling you!

WILLY *(sinking into a chair at a table, with full accusation)*: You're trying to put a knife in me – don't think I don't know
10 what you're doing!

BIFF: All right, phony! Then let's lay it on the line. *(He whips the rubber tube out of his pocket and puts it on the table.)*

HAPPY: You crazy …

LINDA: Biff! *(She moves to grab the hose, but Biff holds it down*
15 *with his hand.)*

BIFF: Leave it there! Don't move it!

WILLY *(not looking at it)*: What is that?

BIFF: You know goddam well what that is.

WILLY *(caged, wanting to escape)*: I never saw that.
20 BIFF: You saw it. The mice didn't bring it into the cellar! What is this supposed to do, make a hero out of you? This supposed to make me sorry for you?

WILLY: Never heard of it.

BIFF: There'll be no pity for you, you hear it? No pity!
25 WILLY *(to Linda)*: You hear the spite!

BIFF: No, you're going to hear the truth – what you are and what I am!

LINDA: Stop it!

WILLY: Spite!
30 HAPPY *(coming down toward Biff)*: You cut it now!

BIFF *(to Happy)*: The man don't know who we are! The man is gonna know! *(To Willy)* We never told the truth for ten minutes in this house!

HAPPY: We always told the truth!
35 BIFF *(turning on him)*: You big blow, are you the assistant buyer? You're one of the two assistants to the assistant, aren't you?

---

4 **to take the rap for sth** *(sl.)* to take the blame for sth that is not your fault – 11 **to lay it on the line** to talk about a problem openly – 14 **to grab** to seize, to take hold of – 19 **caged** forced into a corner like an animal in a cage – 35 **to turn on sb** to speak angrily to sb – 35 **blow** *(sl.)* boaster – 35 **assistant** person who helps the person in charge

HAPPY: Well, I'm practically –
BIFF: You're practically full of it! We all are! And I'm through with
it. *(To Willy.)* Now hear this, Willy, this is me.
WILLY: I know you!
5 BIFF: You know why I had no address for three months? I stole
a suit in Kansas City and I was in jail. *(To Linda, who is sobbing.)* Stop crying. I'm through with it.

(Linda turns away from them, her hands covering her face.)

WILLY: I suppose that's my fault!
10 BIFF: I stole myself out of every good job since high school!
WILLY: And whose fault is that?
BIFF: And I never got anywhere because you blew me so full of
hot air I could never stand taking orders from anybody! That's
whose fault it is!
15 WILLY: I hear that!
LINDA: Don't, Biff!
BIFF: It's goddam time you heard that! I had to be boss big shot
in two weeks, and I'm through with it.
WILLY: Then hang yourself! For spite, hang yourself!
20 BIFF: No! Nobody's hanging himself, Willy! I ran down eleven
flights with a pen in my hand today. And suddenly I stopped,
you hear me? And in the middle of that office building, do you
hear this? I stopped in the middle of that building and I saw
– the sky. I saw the things that I love in this world. The work
25 and the food and time to sit and smoke. And I looked at the
pen and said to myself, what the hell am I grabbing this for?
Why am I trying to become what I don't want to be? What am
I doing in an office, making a contemptuous, begging fool of
myself, when all I want is out there, waiting for me the minute
30 I say I know who I am! Why can't I say that, Willy? *(He tries to
make Willy face him, but Willy pulls away and moves to the
left.)*
WILLY *(with hatred, threateningly)*: The door of your life is wide
open!
35 BIFF: Pop! I'm a dime a dozen, and so are you!

2 **full of it** full of lies and misinformation – 2 **through** finished – 6 **to sob** to weep, to
cry – 10 **I stole myself out of every good job** I lost all my good jobs because of stealing – 12 **you blew me so full of hot air** you made me believe I was such a wonderful
person – 17 **boss big shot** the man on top, the number one – 28 **contemptuous**
[–ˈ– – –] not worthy of respect – 31 **to face** to stand directly in front of sb with one's
face toward the other person – 35 **I'm a dime a dozen.** I'm just an ordinary person. –
35 **dime** ten cents

WILLY *(turning on him now in an uncontrolled outburst)*: I am not a dime a dozen! I am Willy Loman, and you are Biff Loman! *(Biff starts for Willy, but is blocked by Happy. In his fury, Biff seems on the verge of attacking his father.)*

5 BIFF: I am not a leader of men, Willy, and neither are you. You were never anything but a hard-working drummer who landed in the ash can like all the rest of them! I'm one dollar an hour, Willy I tried seven states and couldn't raise it. A buck an hour! Do you gather my meaning? I'm not bringing home
10 any prizes any more, and you're going to stop waiting for me to bring them home!

WILLY *(directly to Biff)*: You vengeful , spiteful mut!

(Biff breaks from Happy. Willy, in fright, starts up the stairs. Biff grabs him.)

15 BIFF *(at the peak of his fury)*: Pop, I'm nothing! I'm nothing, Pop. Can't you understand that? There's no spite in it any more. I'm just what I am, that's all.

(Biff's fury has spent itself, and he breaks down, sobbing, holding on to Willy, who dumbly fumbles for Biff's face.)

20 WILLY *(astonished)*: What're you doing? What're you doing? *(To Linda.)* Why is he crying?

BIFF *(crying, broken)*: Will you let me go, for Christ's sake? Will you take that phony dream and burn it before something happens? *(Struggling to contain himself, he pulls away and
25 moves to the stairs.)* I'll go in the morning. Put him – put him to bed. *(Exhausted, Biff moves up the stairs to his room.)*

WILLY *(after a long pause, astonished, elevated)*: Isn't that – isn't that remarkable? Biff – he likes me!

LINDA: He loves you, Willy!

30 HAPPY *(deeply moved)*: Always did, Pop.

---

7 **ash can** sth waste products are put in; dustbin *(B. E.)* – 7 **I'm one dollar an hour** I'm a low-paid, unskilled worker – 8 **couldn't raise it** couldn't find a better paying job – 9 **to gather** *here:* to understand – 12 **vengeful** wanting to hurt sb when one feels one has been hurt by that person – 12 **spiteful** full of spite – 12 **mut** fool, stupid person – 15 **at the peak** at the highest point – 18 **Biff's fury has spent itself** his anger has lost its force – 19 **dumbly** ['dʌmli] not knowing what one is doing – 19 **to fumble for sth** to feel about uncertainly with one's hands – 24 **to contain oneself** regain control of one's emotions – 27 **elevated** ['eləveɪtɪd] having been made to feel happy – 30 **deeply moved** greatly affected in an emotional way

WILLY: Oh, Biff! *(Staring wildly.)* He cried! Cried to me. *(He is choking with his love, and now cries out his promise.)* That boy – that boy is going to be magnificent!

(Ben appears in the light just outside the kitchen.)

5 BEN: Yes, outstanding, with twenty thousand behind him.

LINDA *(sensing the racing of his mind, fearfully, carefully)*: Now come to bed, Willy. It's all settled now.

WILLY *(finding it difficult not to rush out of the house)*: Yes, we'll sleep. Come on. Go to sleep, Hap.

10 BEN: And it does take a great kind of a man to crack the jungle.

(In accents of dread, Ben's idyllic music starts up.)

HAPPY *(his arm around Linda)*: I'm getting married, Pop, don't forget it. I'm changing everything. I'm gonna run that department before the year is up. You'll see, Mom. *(He kisses her.)*

15 BEN: The jungle is dark but full of diamonds, Willy.

(Willy turns, moves, listening to Ben.)

LINDA: Be good. You're both good boys, just act that way, that's all.

HAPPY: 'Night, Pop. *(He goes upstairs.)*

20 LINDA *(to Willy)*: Come, dear.

BEN *(with greater force)*: One must go in to fetch a diamond out.

WILLY *(to Linda, as he moves slowly along the edge of kitchen, toward the door)*: I just want to get settled down, Linda. Let

25 me sit alone for a little.

LINDA *(almost uttering her fear)*: I want you upstairs.

WILLY *(taking her in his arms)*: In a few minutes, Linda. I couldn't sleep right now. Go on, you look awful tired. *(He kisses her.)*

BEN: Not like an appointment at all. A diamond is rough and

30 hard to the touch.

WILLY: Go on now. I'll be right up.

LINDA: I think this is the only way, Willy.

WILLY: Sure, it's the best thing.

BEN: Best thing!

---

2 **to choke** *here:* to be unable to speak properly because of deep emotions – 3 **magnificent** [mæg'nɪfɪsnt] splendid, remarkable – 6 **the racing of his mind** the thoughts rushing through his head – 10 **to crack** to conquer – 11 **in accents of dread** [dred] in a way which suggests sth unpleasant will happen – 17 **to act** to behave – 24 **settled down** relaxed, calm – 26 **to utter** to express in words

WILLY: The only way. Everything is gonna be – go on, kid, get to bed. You look so tired.

LINDA: Come right up.

WILLY: Two minutes.

5 *(Linda goes into the living room, then reappears in her bedroom. Willy moves just outside the kitchen door.)*

WILLY: Loves me. *(Wonderingly.)* Always loved me. Isn't that a remarkable thing? Ben, he'll worship me for it!

BEN *(with promise)*: It's dark there, but full of diamonds.

10 WILLY: Can you imagine that magnificence with twenty thousand dollars in his pocket?

LINDA *(calling from her room)*: Willy! Come up!

WILLY *(calling into the kitchen)*: Yes! Yes. Coming! It's very smart, you realize that, don't you, sweetheart? Even Ben sees it. I

15 gotta go, baby. 'By! 'By! *(Going over to Ben, almost dancing.)* Imagine? When the mail comes he'll be ahead of Bernard again!

BEN: A perfect proposition all around.

WILLY: Did you see how he cried to me? Oh, if I could kiss him,

20 Ben!

BEN: Time, William, time!

WILLY: Oh, Ben, I always knew one way or another we were gonna make it, Biff and I!

BEN *(looking at his watch)*: The boat. We'll be late. *(He moves*

25 *slowly off into the darkness.)*

WILLY *(elegiacally, turning to the house)*: Now when you kick off, boy, I want a seventy-yard boot, and get right down the field under the ball, and when you hit, hit low and hit hard, because it's important, boy. *(He swings around and faces the*

30 *audience.)* There's all kinds of important people in the stands, and the first thing you know … *(Suddenly realizing he is alone.)* Ben! Ben, where do I …? *(He makes a sudden movement of search.)* Ben, how do I …?

LINDA *(calling)*: Willy, you coming up?

---

8 **to worship** ['wɜːʃɪp] to adore, to love and respect sb – 10 **magnificence** [–'– – –] *here:* great feeling – 13 **smart** clever – 18 **all around** in every way – 26 **elegiacally** [ˌelɪ'dʒaɪəkli] in a sorrowful or sad way – 26 **to kick off** to start a football game – 27 **a boot** *here:* a kick – 27 **get right down the field under the ball** run the whole length of the field while the ball is still in the air – 28 **when you hit** when you hit a player on the other team – 30 **stands** the area in a stadium where the spectators sit

WILLY *(uttering a gasp off fear, whirling about as if to quiet her)*: Sh! *(He turns around as if to find his way; sounds, faces, voices, seem to be swarming in upon him and he flicks at them, crying.)* Sh! Sh! *(Suddenly music, faint and high, stops him. It rises*
5   *in intensity, almost to an unbearable scream. He goes up and down on his toes, and rushes off around the house.)* Shhh!

LINDA: Willy?

(There is no answer. Linda waits. Biff gets up off his bed, He is still in his clothes. Happy sits up. Biff stands listening.)

10   LINDA *(with real fear)*: Willy, answer me! Willy!

(There is the sound of a car starting and moving away at full speed.)

LINDA: No!

BIFF *(rushing down the stairs)*: Pop!

15   *(As the car speeds off, the music crashes down in a frenzy of sound, which becomes the soft pulsation of a single cello string, Biff slowly returns to his bedroom. He and Happy gravely don their jackets. Linda slowly walks out of her room. The music has developed into a dead march. The leaves of day are appear-*
20   *ing over everything. Charley and Bernard, somberly dressed, appear and knock on the kitchen door. Biff and Happy slowly descend the stairs to the kitchen as Charley and Bernard enter. All stop a moment when Linda, in clothes of mourning, bearing a little bunch of roses, comes through the draped doorway*
25   *into the kitchen. She goes to Charley and takes his arm. Now all move toward the audience, through the wall-line of the kitchen. At the limit of the apron, Linda lays down the flowers, kneels, and sits back on her heels. All stare down at the grave.)*

---

1 **gasp** sharp intake of air expressing surprise or shock – 1 **to whirl about** to move around in circles – 3 **to swarm in** to move in one large mass towards sb or sth – 3 **to flick at sth** to make a quick, sharp movement as if to hit sth – 4 **to rise in intensity** to become louder – 15 **to crash down** to suddenly become – 15 **frenzy** wild excitement – 16 **pulsation** vibrating sound – 16 **string** the part of a guitar etc. one moves the fingers over to make sounds – 17 **gravely** solemnly – 17 **to don** to put on – 19 **leaves of day** the leaves as they look during the day – 20 **somberly** in dark colors – 23 **clothes of mourning** clothes worn when sb has died

REQUIEM

CHARLEY: It's getting dark, Linda.

(Linda doesn't react. She stares at the grave.)

BIFF: How about it, Mom? Better get some rest, heh? They'll be closing the gate soon.

5 *(Linda makes no move. Pause.)*

HAPPY *(deeply angered)*: He had no right to do that. There was no necessity for it. We would've helped him.
CHARLEY *(grunting)*: Hmmm.
BIFF: Come along, Mom.
10 LINDA: Why didn't anybody come?
CHARLEY: It was a very nice funeral.
LINDA: But where are all the people he knew? Maybe they blame him.
CHARLEY: Naa. It's a rough world, Linda. They wouldn't blame
15 him.
LINDA: I can't understand it. At this time especially. First time in thirty-five years we were just about free and clear. He only needed a little salary. He was even finished with the dentist.
CHARLEY: No man only needs a little salary.
20 LINDA: I can't understand it.
BIFF: There were a lot of nice days. When he'd come home from a trip; or on Sundays, making the stoop; finishing the cellar; putting on the new porch; when he built the extra bathroom; and put up the garage. You know something, Charley, there's
25 more of him in that front stoop than in all the sales he ever made.
CHARLEY: Yeah. He was a happy man with a batch of cement.
LINDA: He was so wonderful with his hands.
BIFF: He had the wrong dreams. All, all, wrong.
30 HAPPY *(almost ready to fight Biff)*: Don't say that!
BIFF: He never knew who he was.

---

requiem [ˈrekwɪəm] mass for sb who has died – 8 **to grunt** to make a deep rough sound in the throat – 22 **stoop** small staircase leading to a house – 23 **porch** raised platform with a roof, built along the side of a house – 27 **batch** amount;*here:* pile

CHARLEY *(stopping Happy's movement and reply. To Biff)*:
Nobody dast blame this man. You don't understand: Willy was
a salesman. And for a salesman, there is no rock bottom to
the life. He don't put a bolt to a nut, he don't tell you the law or
5 give you medicine. He's a man way out there in the blue, riding on a smile and a shoeshine. And when they start not smiling back – that's an earthquake. And then you get yourself a
couple of spots on your hat, and you're finished. Nobody dast
blame this man. A salesman's got to dream, boy. It comes with
10 the territory.

BIFF: Charley, the man didn't know who he was.

HAPPY *(infuriated)*: Don't say that!

BIFF: Why don't you come with me, Happy?

HAPPY: I'm not licked that easily. I'm staying right in this city,
15 and I'm gonna beat this racket! *(He looks at Biff, his chin set.)*
The Loman Brothers!

BIFF: I know who I am, kid.

HAPPY: All right, boy. I'm gonna show you and everybody else
that Willy Loman did not die in vain. He had a good dream.
20 It's the only dream you can have – to come out number-one
man. He fought it out here, and this is where I'm gonna win
it for him.

BIFF *(with a hopeless glance at Happy, bends toward his mother)*:
Let's go, Mom.

25 LINDA: I'll be with you in a minute. Go on, Charley. *(He hesi-
tates.)* I want to, just for a minute. I never had a chance to say
good-by.

*(Charley moves away, followed by Happy. Biff remains a slight
distance up and left of Linda. She sits there, summoning her-
30 self. The flute begins, not far away, playing behind her speech.)*

LINDA: Forgive me, dear. I can't cry. I don't know what it is, I can't
cry. I don't understand it. Why did you ever do that? Help me
Willy, I can't cry. It seems to me that you're just on another

2 **dast** *(sl.)* dares – 3 **rock bottom** lowest level – 4 **he don't put a bolt to a nut** he
doesn't work with bolts and nuts, he's not a mechanic – 4 **bolt** [bəʊlt] Schraube – 4 **nut**
Mutter – 5 **way out there in the blue** in many different and faraway places – 5 **riding
on a smile and a shoeshine** relying on his friendly behavior and nice clothes – 7 **earthquake** a sudden shaking of the surface of the earth – 9 **it comes with the territory** it's
a part of his job – 10 **territory** area a salesman works in – 12 **infuriated** very angry –
14 **licked** defeated – 15 **I'm gonna beat this racket** I'm going to find a way to be a
success in this difficult business world – 15 **his chin set** his chin unmoving to show he
is determined – 19 **in vain** for no good reason – 29 **up and left** upstage on the left-hand
side – 29 **to summon oneself** to put one's emotions under control

trip. I keep expecting you. Willy, dear, I can't cry. Why did you do it? I search and search and I search, and I can't understand it, Willy. I made the last payment on the house today. Today, dear. And there'll be nobody home. *(A sob rises in her throat.)*
5   We're free and clear. *(Sobbing more fully released.)* We're free. *(Biff comes slowly toward her.)* We're free … We're free …

(Biff lifts her to her feet and moves out up right with her in his arms. Linda sobs quietly. Bernard and Charley come together and follow them, followed by Happy. Only the music of the
10   *flute is left on the darkening stage as over the house the hard towers of the apartment buildings rise into sharp focus, and the curtain falls.)*

---

5 **clear** with no debts – 5 **released** no longer held back – 11 **to rise into sharp focus** to become very clear and distinct

Assignments to Be Completed While Reading the Play

I. The plot.
   1. Write a scene-by-scene summary of the plot. Be sure to include the "flashbacks" and the retrospective parts with the linear plot.
   2. How are the "flashbacks" inserted into the linear plot?
   3. What purpose do the "flashbacks" serve?
   4. Are there any climaxes or turning points?

II. The characters
   1. How do the characters evaluate themselves and how do the other characters evaluate them? Pay special attention to what is said about Willy.
   2. Observe the inflection, diction, and gestures of the characters in different situations.
   3. Compare Willy with Howard, Charley, and Ben. Are any of them foils or antagonists?
   4. Compare Biff and Happy with Bernard.
   5. Do any of the characters change in the course of the play?
   6. What is Linda's role in the play?

III. The stage sets
   1. What is the playwright trying to evoke with the detailed stage directions at the beginning of the play?
   2. Examine the use of music and sound effects.
   3. Observe the use of props within the context of the action.

IV. The themes
   1. Analyse Willy's, Biff's, and Happy's dreams and aspirations. How are country and city contrasted in them?
   2. What is the relationship between the various characters' dreams and aspirations, and the reality they live in?
   3. What are the conflicts in the drama? What are their causes?
   4. Contrast and compare Willy's, Howard's, Charley's, and Ben's attitudes towards personal and business ethics.
   5. Observe the relationship between father and son.

6. Consider the following statements about Willy. Find arguments which support each statement.

LINDA: The man is exhausted.

BIFF: I know he's a fake.

CHARLEY: Willy, when are you going to grow up?

MATERIAL FOR FURTHER STUDY

Arthur Miller and the Critics

1. Old Glamour, New Gloom

It would seem that the success of Arthur Miller's, or Elia Kazan's *Death of a Salesman* has been due largely to the feeling of depression with which one makes for the exit. The idea is that anything that can make you feel that glum must be good [...].

5 [Willy Loman] is the common man, and something or other has gone terribly wrong. The point is, what and why. At first blush the answer seems fairly simple. Willy has a fatal flaw. He lives in a dream world; he can't face reality; he has always had excuses for his own failures ("the shop was closed for inventory") and
10 has ruined Biffs life by indulging him all through his childhood in any whim including theft. It is a good theme. But it turns out not only that the author is saying a good deal more than this, but that he is also either very unclear as to his further meanings, or very anxious to present them and evade responsibility for them
15 at the same time. It is, of course, the capitalist system that has done Willy in; the scene in which he is brutally fired after some forty years with the firm comes straight from the party line literature of the 'thirties; and the idea emerges lucidly enough through all the confused motivations of the play that it is our
20 particular form of money economy that has bred the absurdly false ideals of both father and sons. It emerges, however, like a succession of shots from a duck blind. Immediately after every crack the playwright withdraws behind an air of pseudo-uni-

---

glamour exciting attractiveness – **gloom** feeling of despair – 1 **Elia Kazan** the director of the first production *of Death of a Salesman* – 3 **to make for** to walk towards – 4 **glum** cheerless, sad – 6 **at first blush** at first sight – 7 **fatal flaw** weakness which will be the downfall of the person or thing, tragic flaw – 9 **for inventory** in order to check what goods and materials were in the shop – 10 **to indulge** to always let sb have or do what he wants – 11 **whim** a sudden unexpected and usually short-lived desire – 14 **to evade** to avoid – 16 **to do sb in** to destroy or kill sb – 17 **party line** official view and policies of a political party, here the Communist party – 18 **to emerge** to come into view, appear – 18 **lucidly** clearly – 20 **to breed, bred, bred** *here:* to cause to develop – 21 **succession** a number of things following each other – 22 **duck blind** structure behind which a hunter hides so as to shoot down ducks – 23 **crack** *here:* shot – 23 **air** appearance – 23 **pseudo** ['sjuːdəʊ] not real, false – 23 **universality** [– – –'– – –] the quality of being true for all times not just the present

117

versality, and hurries to present some cruelty or misfortune due either to Willy's own weakness, as when he refuses his friend's offer of a job after he has been fired, or gratuitously from some other source, as in the quite unbelievable scene of the two sons
5 walking out on their father in the restaurant. In the end, after so much heaping of insult on injury, all one really knows about Willy Loman is that if the system doesn't kick him in the teeth he will do it himself – a well-known if wearisome tendency, that in itself might have dramatic possibilities, but that is neither par-
10 ticularly associated with salesmen nor adapted to the purposes of this play.

What it does lend itself to in this case is an intellectual mud-dle and a lack of candor that regardless of Mr. Miller's conscious intent are the main earmark of contemporary fellow-traveling.
15 What used to be a roar has become a whine, and this particular piece of whining has been so expertly put over that it has been able to pass for something else, but behind all the fancy staging the old basic clumsiness and lack of humor are there. To be sure there are a few moments of ordinary Broadway sprightliness, as
20 in the matter of the icebox, or Hap's little performance with the girls in the restaurant, but these are in passing.

[…] As for the clumsiness, it shows not only in the large aspects of the play but, rather surprisingly considering the gen-eral technical excellence of the job in a number of small ones
25 too. That the much-stressed point of Willy's being deprived of working with his hands, and of his pride in that, is not a spe-cific reflection on the money standards which are central to the play's action, but, as remarked on by many writers over the last hundred years, has to do with modern mechanized society
30 in whatever form, could perhaps be passed over. But nothing

---

3 **gratuitous** [grə'tjuːɪtəs] without any apparent reason – 6 **to heap** to pile up, to place things one on top of the other – 6 **to heap insult on injury** a variation on the expression "to add insult to injury," meaning to make an already bad situation even worse – 7 **the system** the existing social, political, and economic system, *here:* Capital-ism – 8 **wearisome** tiring and boring – 10 **adapted to** suited to, fitting – 12 **to lend itself to** to be suitable for – 12 **muddle** confusion – 13 **candor** openness, frankness – 14 **ear-mark** characteristic – 14 **contemporary** present-day – 14 **fellow-traveling** sympathiz-ing with the beliefs of the Communist party – 16 **whine** a long high sound of pain or complaining – 16 **to put sth over** to present sth effectively often with the purpose of deceiving – 17 **fancy** decorative, elaborate – 17 **staging** the production and direction of a play – 19 **Broadway** commercial theater district in New York City; *here:* characteristic of commercial theater – 19 **sprightliness** liveliness, cheerfulness – 21 **in passing** not of central importance (in the play) – 25 **to deprive sb of sth** to prevent sb from having or doing sth – 27 **a reflection on** a (critical) comment on

excuses the triteness and pseudo-psychoanalytic nature of the Boston scene, dragged in to explain Biff's failures, though he would have been far better perceived as a contemporary character without it. It is also annoying not to know what the sales-
5 man sells, and whether or not the insurance is going to be paid after his death, and to have the wife say in her final speech that they were just getting out of debt, with no previous explanation of how, and when in fact we have just seen Willy getting further into debt.

10 These are details, but they indicate something of the speciousness of the play, which manages at every point to obscure both the real tragedy and the real comedy of the material. Willy is presumed to be losing his mind because he talks to himself, which permits the long series of flashbacks that give the play its
15 illusion of liveliness, a form of madness that can at least, in the case, be called convenient; but all of us have seen and probably most of us have experienced delusions wilder and more illuminating than this. In the picture of Biff's unhappy restlessness Mr. Miller gives an impression of contemporaneity, but that is
20 all; the true malaise of men of thirty now is a great deal more terrible than what happens to anyone in this play, and would not be a subject for a Broadway success.

"Old Glamour, New Gloom" by Eleanor Clark first appeared in *Partisan Review*, Vol. XVI, No. 6 (June 1949), pp. 631–635. Reprinted by permission of *Partisan Review* and Eleanor Clark.

2. Audience Spellbound by Prize Play of 1949

Here's my true report that, yesterday at the Morosco, the first-night congregation made no effort to leave the theatre at
25 the final curtain-fall of Arthur Miller's *Death of a Salesman*. It's

1 **triteness** dullness, lack of originality – 1 **psycho-analytic** [ˌsaɪkəʊˌnəˈlɪtɪk] analyzing thoughts and feelings following Sigmund Freud's theory of psychology – 2 **to drag sth in** *here:* to include sth at all costs without it really fitting the context – 3 **to perceive** *here:* to understand – 10 **speciousness** [ˈspiːʃəsnəs]
appearance of being true when in fact being false – 11 **to obscure** to hide from view – 13 **to presume** to assume – 17 **delusion** sth that is falsely believed because of an abnormal mental state – 17 **illuminating** making sth clear and understandable – 19 **contemporaneity** being of the present day – 20 **malaise** [mɒˈleɪz] a vague feeling of dissatisfaction, uneasiness – 22 **spellbound** fascinated – 22 **prize play** *here:* play that is expected to win the Pulitzer Prize (a respected American prize for literature) – 23 **Morosco** a Broadway theater – 24 **congregation** group of people attending a church*service, here:* audience

meant to make known to you the prevailing emotional impact of the new play by the author of *All My Sons*.

As a theatre reporter I'm telling you how that first-night congregation remained in its seats beyond the final curtain-fall. For 5 a period somewhat shorter than it seemed, an expectant silence hung over the crowded auditorium. Then, believe me, tumultuous appreciation shattered the hushed expectancy.

It was, and will remain, one of the lasting rewards that I, as a professional theatregoer, have received in a long full life of pro- 10 fessional theatregoing. In *Death of a Salesman*, Arthur Miller had given that first-night congregation no ordinary new play to praise, to damn, or to ignore.

This, his most iconoclastic composition, is not easy on its congregation, first-night or later on. In writing what he wants 15 to write, he has asked – demanded, rather – your sympathy as a fellow member of the bedeviled human race and your attention as an intelligent collaborator as well.

These, with everything else that's good, the author of *Death of a Salesman* received wholeheartedly last night. The play's play- 20 wright and playgoers were worthy of each other.

If Everyman will forgive me, in Arthur Miller's Salesman there's much of Everyman. Bothered, bewildered, but mostly bedeviled, as Willy Loman is, he's not a great deal different from the majority of his contemporaries. He, even as you and I, builds 25 himself a shaky shelter of illusion.

You've the author's word that the motif of *Death of a Salesman* is the growth of illusion in even the most commonplace of mortals. In Willy Loman, the illusionist of the title, the individual is destroyed. And his progeny, Biff and Happy, are wrecked 30 upon the rocks of reality. Willy has created an image of himself which fails to correspond with Willy Loman as he is. According to the playwright, it's the size of the discrepancy that matters. In

1 **prevailing** predominant, most noticeable – 1 **impact** effect – 4 **beyond** *here:* after – 6 **auditorium** area where the audience sits in a theater – 6 **tumultuous** [tuːˈmʌltʃʊəs] very noisy – 6 **tumultuous appreciation** loud clapping and shouting indicating a positive response – 7 **to shatter** to break suddenly and usually into many pieces – 7 **hushed** silent, quiet – 13 **iconoclastic** [aɪˌkɒnəˈklɔstɪk] attacking traditional beliefs and traditions – 13 **composition** literary work – 13 **to be easy on** to be pleasant or relaxing to sb, to demand little effort from – 16 **fellow** being of the same kind – 16 **bedeviled** [bɪˈdevəld] tormented, frustrated – 17 **collaborator** sb who works together with sb else, partner – 19 **wholeheart-edly** completely and enthusiastically – 21 **Everyman** the "common man," the average citizen – 22 **bothered** troubled – 22 **bewildered** [bɪˈwɪldəd] confused, puzzled – 24 **contemporary** person living in the same period of time – 25 **shelter** small building or covered place that provides protection – 26 **motif** theme – 27 **commonplace** ordinary – 28 **mortal** human being, as opposed to a god – 29 **progeny** [ˈprɒdʒəni] descendants, children –31 **to correspond with** to match (with) – 32 **discrepancy** [– – – –] difference, lack of agreement

Salesman Loman, the discrepancy is so great that it finally slays him. Ironically, by his own unsteady hand.

In *Death of a Salesman,* the present and the past of Willy Loman exist concurrently – the "stream of consciousness" idea
5 – until they collide in climax. Isn't it true that the Willy Lomans of this world are their own worst tragedy? At the Morosco, only Linda Loman can foresee the end.

And she, as wife and mother, is powerless to prevent it. This, to me, is the play's most tragic tragedy. She, too, is the play's
10 most poignant figure. Not soon shall I forget her!

By Robert Garland from *The New York Journal-American*, February 11, 1949, p. 24.

3. *Past and Present in* Death of a Salesman

The *Salesman* image was from the beginning absorbed with the concept that nothing in life comes "next" but that everything exists together and at the same time within us; that there is no past to be "brought forward" in a human being, but that he is his
15 past at every moment and that the present is merely that which his past is capable of noticing and smelling and reacting to.

I wished to create a form which, in itself as a form, would literally be the process of Willy Loman's way of mind […] As I look at the play now its form seems the form of a confession, for that
20 is how it is told, now speaking of what happened yesterday, then suddenly following some connection to a time twenty years ago, then leaping even further back and then returning to the present and even speculating about the future.

[…] The structure of events and the nature of its form are also
25 the direct reflection of Willy Loman's way of thinking at this moment of his life. He was the kind of man you see muttering to himself on a subway, decently dressed, on his way home or to the office, perfectly integrated with his surroundings excepting that unlike other people he can no longer restrain the power

1 **to slay** to destroy, to kill – 2 **unsteady** shaky – 4 **concurrently** at the same time –
4 **stream of consciousness** *in literature* the description of the continuous flow of a
character's thoughts – 5 **to collide** to come together violently – 10 **poignant** ['pɔɪnjənt]
causing a feeling of sympathy – 11 **image** picture in the mind, how sb imagines sth to
be – 11 **absorbed with** *here:* concerned with – 12 **concept** idea – 17 **literally** really, actually – 19 **confession** act of admitting one has done sth wrong – 22 **to leap** to jump –
26 **to mutter** to speak quietly and unclearly so that one cannot be easily heard – 27 **on
a subway** on a train in the New York underground – 29 **to restrain** to hold back, to
control

of his experience from disrupting the superficial sociality of his behavior. Consequently he is working on two logics which often collide. For instance, if he meets his son Happy while in the midst of some memory in which Happy disappointed him,
5   he is instantly furious at Happy, despite the fact that Happy at this particular moment deeply desires to be of use to him. [...]

The ability of people to down their past is normal, and without it we could have no comprehensible communication among men. In the hands of writers who see it as an easy way to
10 elicit anterior information in a play it becomes merely a flashback. There are no flashbacks in this play but only a mobile concurrency of past and present, and this, again, because in his desperation to justify his life Willy Loman has destroyed the boundaries between now and then.

From the author's introduction to *Arthur Miller's Collected Plays*, New York: Viking, *1957, pp. 23-26.* Copyright © 1957 by Arthur Miller. Reprinted by permission of International Creative Management, Inc.

4. Death of a Salesman *and the Public*

15 A great deal has been said and written about what *Death of a Salesman is* supposed to signify, both psychologically and from the socio-political viewpoints. For instance, in one periodical of the far Right it was called a "time bomb expertly placed under the edifice of Americanism," while the *Daily Worker* reviewer
20 thought it entirely decadent. In Catholic Spain it ran longer than any modern play and it has been refused production in Russia but not, from time to time, in certain satellite countries, depending on the direction and velocity of the wind. The Spanish press, thoroughly controlled by Catholic orthodoxy, regarded

---

1 **to disrupt** to upset the order of, to throw into confusion – 1 **superficial** [ˌsuːpəˈfɪʃl] not very deep, only on the surface – 1 **sociality** normal way of acting as a member of society – 2 **he is working on two logics** he is following two lines of thought or reasoning – 7 **to down** *here:* to suppress, to make oneself forget – 8 **comprehensible** clear, meaningful – 10 **to elicit** to bring out – 10 **anterior** from an earlier time – 11 **mobile** (freely) moving – 12 **concurrency** happening at the same time – 16 **to signify** to mean – 17 **periodical** magazine that appears regularly – 19 **edifice** [ˈedɪfɪs] impressive building – 19 **Americanism** the American economic and political system –19 **Daily Worker** a Communist newspaper – 19 **reviewer** person who writes critical reports about literary works or performances – 22 **satellite country** country that is politically dominated by another, esp. country in eastern Europe when the Soviet Union still existed – 23 **the direction and velocity of the wind** *here:* the political views of the regime at a particular time

the play as commendable proof of the spirit's death where there is no God. In America, even as it was being cannonaded as a piece of Communist propaganda, two of the largest manufacturing corporations in the country invited me to address their
5 sales organizations in conventions assembled, while the road company was here and there picketed by the Catholic War Veterans and the American Legion. […] One organization of salesmen raised me up nearly to patron-sainthood, and another, a national sales managers' group, complained that the difficulty
10 of recruiting salesmen was directly traceable to the play. When the movie was made, the producing company got so frightened it produced a sort of trailer to be shown before the picture, a documentary short film which demonstrated how exceptional Willy Loman was; how necessary selling is to the economy; how
15 secure the salesman's life really is; how idiotic, in short, was the feature film they had just spent more than a million dollars to produce. Fright does odd things to people.

[…] The letters from women made it clear that the central character of the play was Linda; sons saw the entire action
20 revolving around Biff or Happy, and fathers wanted advice, in effect, on how to avoid parricide. Probably the most succinct reaction to the play was voiced by a man who, on leaving the theater, said, "I always said that New England territory was no damned good." This, at least, was a fact.
25 That I have and had not the slightest interest in the selling profession is probably unbelievable to most people, and I very early gave up trying even to say so. And when asked what Willy was selling, what was in his bags, I could only reply, "Himself."

From the author's introduction to *Arthur Miller's Collected Plays*, New York: Viking, 1957, pp. 27-28. Copyright © 1957 by Arthur Miller. Reprinted by permission of International Creative Management, Inc.

1 **commendable** which deserves praise – 2 **to cannonade** *here:* to attack fiercely –
5 **convention** large gathering of people belonging to an organization – 5 **road company** group of actors traveling from town to town to give performances of a play – 6 **to picket** to stand as a group outside a building to protest against sth and to try to stop others from entering – 6 **Catholic War Veterans** organization for Roman Catholics who fought in wars for America – 7 **the American Legion** an organization open to anyone who fought in a war for America, often criticized for being too pro-military – 8 **patron-sainthood** state of being the patron saint (Schutzheiliger) – 10 **to recruit** [rɪˈkruːt] to find and employ sb to do a certain job – 10 **to be traceable to** to be caused by, to be a consequence of – 12 **trailer** short film advertising a full-length film – 13 **exceptional** uncommon – 16 **feature film** major full-length film – 17 **odd** strange – 20 **in effect** in fact, in reality – 21 **parricide** the act of murdering one's father – 21 **succinct** [səkˈsɪŋkt] clearly expressed in a few words – 22 **to voice** to express – 25 **slight** very small

5. A Tragic Hero?

The play was always heroic to me, and in later years the academy's charge that Willy lacked the "stature" for the tragic hero
seemed incredible to me. I had not understood that these matters are measured by Greco-Elizabethan paragraphs which
5   hold no mention of insurance payments, front porches, refrigerator fan belts, steering knuckles, Chevrolets, and visions seen
not through the portals of Delphi but in the blue flame of the
hot-water heater. How could "Tragedy" make people weep, of
all things?

10   I set out not to "write a tragedy" in this play, but to show the
truth as I saw it. However, some of the attacks upon it as a pseu-
do-tragedy contain ideas so misleading, and in some cases so
laughable, that it might be in place here to deal with a few of
them.

15   Aristotle having spoken of a fall from the heights, it goes
without saying that someone of the common mold cannot be
a fit tragic hero. It is now many centuries since Aristotle lived.
There is no more reason for falling down in a faint before his
Poetics than before Euclid's geometry, which has been amended
20   numerous times by men with new insights; nor, for that matter,
would I choose to have my illnesses diagnosed by Hippocrates
rather than the most ordinary graduate of an American medical
school, despite the Greek's genius. Things do change, and even
a genius is limited by his time and the nature of his society.

25   I would deny, on grounds of simple logic, this one of Aristotle's contentions if only because he lived in a slave society. When

---

1 **academy** [əˈkædəmi] university professors widely accepted as authorities – 2 **charge**
accusation, criticism – 2 **stature** [ˈstætʃə] status, importance – 4 **Greco-Elizabethan** having to do with the ancient Greeks or the time of Elizabeth I (16th and early 17th centuries) – 4 **paragraph** *here:* rule, regulation – 5 **to hold** to contain – 6 **steering knuckle**
device on a steering wheel that helps the driver to drive straight ahead – 6 **Chevrolet**
[ˌʃevrəˈleɪ] a low-priced car – 7 **portal** [ˈ– –] large impressive entrance – 7 **Delphi** [ˈdelfaɪ]
in ancient times a place where priestesses in a dreamlike state had visions about the
future – 8 **to weep** to cry – 13 **in place** the right place, appropriate – 15 **Aristotle** Greek
philosopher (384-322 B.C.) – 16 **sb of the common mold** an ordinary person – 17 **fit**
suitable – 18 **in a faint** completely unconscious;*here:* with excessive respect – 19 **Poetics** a work by Aristotle dealing with the definition of tragedy – 19 **Euclid** Greek math-
ematician of the third century B.C. known for his system of geometry – 19 **to amend**
to adapt, update – 20 **for that matter** as far as that is concerned – 21 **Hippocrates**
[hɪˈpɒkrətiːz] Greek doctor of medicine (460-377 B.C.) – 22 **graduate** person who has
successfully completed a course of study at a university or college – 25 **on grounds of**
on the basis of contention argument, opinion – 26 **if only because** und sei es nur weil

a vast number of people are divested of alternatives, as slaves are, it is rather inevitable that one will not be able to imagine drama, let alone tragedy, as being possible for any but the high ranks of society. There is a legitimate question of stature here, but none of rank, which is so often confused with it. So long as the hero may be said to have had alternatives of a magnitude to have materially changed the course of his life, it seems to me that in this respect at least, he cannot be debarred from the heroic role […]

It was not out of any deference to a tragic definition that Willy Loman is filled with a joy, however broken-hearted, as he approaches his end, but simply that my sense of his character dictated his joy, and even what I felt was an exultation. In terms of his character, he has achieved a very powerful piece of knowledge, which is that he is loved by his son and has been embraced by him and forgiven. In this he is given his existence, so to speak his fatherhood, for which he has always striven and which until now he could not achieve. That he is unable to take this victory thoroughly to his heart, that it closes the circle for him and propels him to his death, is the wage of his sin, which was to have committed himself so completely to the counterfeits of dignity and the false coinage embodied in his idea of success that he can prove his existence only by bestowing "power" on his posterity, a power deriving from the sale of his last asset, himself, for the price of his insurance policy.

I must confess here to a miscalculation, however. I did not realize while writing the play that so many people in the world

1 **vast** great – 1 **to divest sb of sth** to take sth away from sb – 2 **inevitable** [–ˈ– – – –] certain to happen – 4 **legitimate** [lɪˈdʒɪtɪmət] reasonable, justified – 6 **magnitude** Größenordnung – 7 **materially** greatly, substantially – 8 **to be debarred from** to be excluded from – 10 **out of** because of – 10 **deference to** [ˈdefrəns] polite respect for – 13 **to dictate** to make necessary – 13 **exultation** great joy – 13 **in terms of** with respect to, considering – 15 **to embrace** to put one's arms around sb to show one's love – 17 **to strive for sth** to make a great effort to get sth – 18 **to take sth to one's heart** *here:* to accept sth fully and feel satisfied as a result – 19 **to propel** [–ˈ–] to drive forward, to cause to move in a particular direction – 20 **sin** Sünde – 24 **wage of his sin** refers to Romans 6:23: "The wages of sin is death." – 21 **to commit oneself to sth** to bind oneself to sth – 21 **counterfeit** [ˈkaʊntəfɪt] imitation of sth meant to make you believe it is the real thing – 22 **coinage** metal money, coins – 22 **false coinage** *(fig.)* false values – 22 **embodied in** included, contained in – 23 **to bestow** [bɪˈstəʊ] to present as a gift – 23 **posterity** [pɒsˈterəti] descendants, future generations – 24 **to derive from** to come from, to originate from – 24 **asset** [ˈæset] anything that one owns that can be turned into cash – 26 **to confess** to admit – 26 **miscalculation** mistake in judgment

do not see as clearly, or would not admit, as I thought they must, how futile most lives are; so there could be no hope of consoling the audience for the death of this man. I did not realize either how few would be impressed by the fact that this man is actu-
5 ally a very brave spirit who cannot settle for half but must pursue his dream of himself to the end. Finally, I thought it must be clear, even obvious, that this was no dumb brute heading mindlessly to his catastrophe.

I have no need to be Willy's advocate before the jury which
10 decides who is and who is not a tragic hero. I am merely noting that the lingering ponderousness of so many ancient definitions has blinded students and critics to the facts before them, and not only in regard to this play. Had Willy been unaware of his separation from values that endure he would have died con-
15 tentedly while polishing his car, probably on a Sunday afternoon with the ball game coming over the radio. But he was agonized by his awareness of being in a false position, so constantly haunted by the hollowness of all he had placed his faith in, so aware, in short, that he must somehow be filled in his spirit or
20 fly apart, that he staked his very life on the ultimate assertion. That he had not the intellectual fluency to verbalize his situation is not the same thing as saying that he lacked awareness, even an overly intensified consciousness that the life he had made was without form and inner meaning.

From the author's introduction to *Arthur Miller's Collected Plays*, New York: Viking, 1957, pp. 31-32, 34-35. Copyright © 1957 by Arthur Miller. Reprinted by permission of International Creative Management, Inc.

2 **futile** ['fjuːtl] useless, pointless – 2 **to console** to comfort, to offer sympathy to sb who is unhappy or disappointed – 5 **to settle for sth** to accept less than one hoped for – 7 **brute** person lacking intelligence or reason – 8 **mindlessly** foolishly, unthinkingly – 9 **advocate** person who defends sb in court – 9 **jury** group of people in a court of law who decide whether sb is guilty – 11 **to linger** ['lɪŋgə] to remain longer than necessary – 11 **ponderousness** ['pɒndərəsnəs] quality of being dull and unable to move or change, usually because of too much weight – 13 **in regard to** concerning – 13 **to be unaware** not to know or realize – 14 **to endure** to continue to exist without changing – 16 **to be agonized** ['ægənaɪzd] to be tormented, to suffer mentally – 17 **awareness** state of having knowledge or realization – 18 **to be haunted by sth** to be constantly troubled by sth – 18 **hollowness** emptiness – 18 **faith** trust and belief – 20 **to fly apart** to break down – 20 **to stake** to risk, to bet – 20 **his very life** even his own life – 20 **ultimate** most extreme, last – 20 **assertion** affirmation, positive declaration – 21 **fluency** ability to express oneself well – 21 **to verbalize** to express one's ideas in words – 23 **overly** excessively, in an exaggerated way – 23 **intensified** greater in strength – 23 **consciousness** ['kɒnʃəsnəs] awareness

6. A New Broadway Production of the Play

The premiere of Death of a Salesman *in 1949 was dominated by the actor Lee J. Cobb (1911-1976) who played the role of Willy Loman. Thirty-five years later, in 1984, a new production of the play opened on Broadway, starring Dustin Hoffman. A film ver-*
5 *sion, based on this new Broadway production and directed by Volker Schlöndorff, was broadcast by CBS television in September 1985.*

The primary reason for the production's success out of town, in addition to Hoffman's magnetism, is, of course, the remarkable
10 durability of the play itself. Thirty-five years ago, in its Broadway premiere, it immediately established Miller in the front rank of American dramatists. When it is revived […] people are moved again to pay attention to the plight of Willy Loman, a salesman "riding on a smile and a shoeshine."
15 Willy's story is, as Miller intended, that of a common man devoted to, and ultimately defeated by, a false system of values that Willy honors as a hallmark of free enterprise. Approached from the perspective of today's computerized society, in which both machines and men bring about their own obsolescence,
20 and salesmanship is a contest waged on a corporate and political level, Miller's lament for the loss of individualism has a renewed relevance. "Salesman" also deals poetically with timeless questions of family, paternal expectations and filial assertiveness. As Willy and Biff, father and son, try to reach across a
25 chasm of regret and disappointment in one another, they stir audiences to compassionate recognition.

As for Arthur Miller, he has been patiently waiting for Hoffman to grow into the role of Willy Loman. And to anyone who

8 **primary** main – 8 **out of town** *here:* away from Broadway, outside of New York (new plays are often staged out of town before coming to Broadway to test public opinion) – 10 **durability** [͵– –ˈ– – –] ability to last a long time – 11 **in the front rank** as one of the best – 12 **to revive** to bring back to life – 13 **plight** difficult situation – 16 **to be devoted to** to give all of oneself to – 16 **ultimately** in the end – 17 **hallmark** typical characteristic indicating sth is genuine – 17 **free enterprise** economic system in which private businesses can compete with each other without government interference – 17 **approached** *here:* looked at – 19 **obsolescence** [͵ɒbsəˈlesns] process of becoming obsolete, i.e. no longer useful – 20 **salesmanship** ability to sell – 20 **to wage** to engage in, to participate in – 20 **corporate** having to do with big business – 21 **lament** [ləˈment] expression of sorrow – 23 **paternal** [–ˈ– –] fatherly – 23 **filial** of a son or daughter – 23 **assertiveness** tendency to express an independent opinion – 25 **chasm** [kɒzm] deep opening – 25 **to stir** to affect the emotions – 26 **compassionate** feeling sorrow or pity for the suffering of others

thinks that, at 46, the actor is still too young, the playwright is quick to point out that the late Lee J. Cobb originated the role when he was 37. In addition, Miller conceived of Willy as a little man, and, in fact, altered a few lines of dialogue to accommo-
5 date Cobb's burly physique. In the original script, Willy was referred to as "a shrimp," which became, in Cobb's version, "a walrus." Once again Willy is a "shrimp."

There are, of course, other basic differences between Cobb and Hoffman. As Miller says, "Cobb was born old. He was lugu-
10 brious and depressed. Dustin has always been chipper and full of energy." If Cobb had a paternal aura, Hoffman will, for many people, remain the son, Benjamin, home from college in "The Graduate." Even when he played a father, as in "Kramer vs . Kramer," the characterization was that of a young husband
15 learning to act as a parent. On the other hand, as a character actor, he has often played far older than his years – his oldest so far was as the 121-year-old Indian scout in "Little Big Man." More important, he feels an emotional identification with the plays of Miller and the world of Willy Loman. Ever since he read
20 the Play – at the age of 17 – he has had "a fix" on the character, much of that based on parallels he sees within his own family. [...]

During this period [of finding actors for the various parts], Hoffman and Miller became closer. "After about two months,
25 I started to say the lines with his rhythms." He got out his copy of the "Salesman" record and played Miller's spoken introduction again and again, and then, against everyone's advice, he left the record on and heard Lee J. Cobb's performance. "I hadn't listened to it since we cut the record," Hoffman said. "It recalled
30 to me all the times I had hung around rehearsal and watched him. His Willy was like Rodin, and it depressed me." Gradually, he realized, "I don't have his kind of power, his guns – and that

2 **late** who is now dead (esp. said of sb who has died recently) – 3 **to conceive of** to form an idea in the mind – 4 **to alter** to change – 4 **to accommodate sth, sb** to adjust sth to make it suitable for sth, sb – 5 **burly** ['bɜːli] heavy, muscular – 5 **physique** [fɪ'ziːk] body, physical statute – 7 **walrus** (Walross) *here:* large person – 7 **shrimp** a very short and lean person – 9 **lugubrious** [lə'guːbriəs] gloomy, not cheerful – 10 **chipper** active and cheerful – 11 **aura** quality – 13 **The Graduate** film (1967) which started Dustin Hoffman on his career; German title: Die Reifeprüfung – 15 **character actor** actor who plays the roles of characters who have distinctive and unusual characteristics – 20 **fix** *here:* an extremely strong and constant interest in – 29 **to cut a record** to make a record – 29 **to recall** to bring back to sb's mind – 30 **to hang around** to stand around doing nothing important – 30 **rehearsal** [rɪ'hɜːsl] practice session of sth to be performed publicly – 31 **Rodin** (1840-1917) French sculptor, known for his muscular figures – 32 **guns** *here:* forcefulness

was a liberating thing. I was going toward the opposite. Instead of this 'walrus,' I was going to be a spitfire."

When his friend the playwright Murray Schisgal asked him if he were going to play the role with a potbelly, he said, "No, I'm
5 going to lose weight." As he explained: "I want to be just skin and bones. Willy has been trying to kill himself for six months. The play is the last 24 hours in his life. Willy can't sleep, can't eat. He's wired."

The play begins early in the morning with Willy suddenly
10 coming home in the middle of a selling trip. "He's never aborted a trip before. That's like an actor not finishing a play, walking off the stage in the first act. If there's one word that sums up Willy, it's preoccupation. What's very important to him is to go out a winner. He's got to go right at the moment when he's decided
15 that Biff loves him. It's like saying, 'The audience likes me.' Go out to a standing ovation."

As Miller said about Hoffman's approach: "He has to know with his brain and his belly what the center of the dramatic issue is. He peels it off like an onion, getting to the middle of the
20 middle. Cobb was led to it by Kazan," he added, referring to the director Elia Kazan. "He had a marvelous voice and looked great and he would always lean on his equipment to get him through narrow spaces. Dustin can't. He has that kind of feisty quickness that I always associated with Willy, changing directions like
25 a sailboat in the middle of a lake with the wind blowing in all directions. He's a cocky little guy overwhelmed by the size of the world and trying to climb up to the top of the mountain. Dustin will create a new Willy. It ain't going to be the other one. It'll be his Willy."

From "Dustin Hoffman's 'Salesman'" by Mel Gussow, *The New York Times Magazine*, March 18, 1984, pp. 38, 46, 48. Copyright © 1984 by the New York Times Company. Reprinted by permission.

2 **spitfire** highly excitable person – 4 **potbelly** large stomach – 8 **wired** *here:* extremely excitable – 10 **to abort** to break off before finishing sth – 12 **to sum up** to describe in a few words, summarize – 13 **preoccupation** state of having one's mind completely concerned with sth and so not being able to concentrate on other things – 13 **to go out** *here:* to die – 16 **standing ovation** enthusiastic applause from the audience standing up – 17 **approach** method of dealing with sth – 19 **issue** point in question – 19 **to peel** to take away the outside layer of sth – 22 **to lean on his equipment** *here:* to rely upon his voice and appearance – 23 **narrow spaces** *here:* difficult situations – 23 **feisty** ['faɪsti] excitable, full of nervous energy – 26 **cocky** very self-confident – 26 **overwhelmed** overpowered – 28 **ain't** *(sl.)* isn't

Success, Happiness, and the American Dream

7. Love and Success

For the parents the child's relative success gives the answer to
the question: "Have I been a good American parent? Have I
produced and equipped a child who can hold his own, make
good, amount to something, reach heights which I cannot?" But
5 to the child (and so to the adult) its own success means much
more than that. "Am I successful?" comes to mean "Am I loved?"
For from the very beginning, the mother's unqualified love and
approval have been given to her child in proportion to its success. By adolescence most Americans have inextricably con-
10 fused the two ideas: to be successful is to be loved, to be loved is
to be successful. This confusion is even given a quasi-theologi-
cal sanction, derived from the puritanism of New England as
diffused by the schoolteachers: worldly success is an outward
and visible sign of the love of God, of Providence; to be a failure
15 signifies that one is unloved by God, that one has sinned, or, at
the least, has not tried hard enough. [...]
   In childhood and youth good grades in school were rewarded
by the love and praise of the parents, especially the mother; and
consequently good grades quickly came to symbolize a promise
20 of love. Dollars in adult life would seem to have something of
the same function, signs that one is worthy of love and should
receive it. And just as most Americans are insatiable for the personal signs of friendship and love, so do many appear insatiable for the dollars which are also the promissory notes of love.
25 In the biographies of many of the conspicuously successful,
a recurring theme is the stern upbringing or harsh childhood
which forced them early to seek success. [...]

---

3 **to equip** to provide what is necessary – 3 **to hold one's own** to be able to look
after oneself – 3 **to make good** to be successful – 4 **to amount to sth** to become sb
people can respect – 6 **to come to mean** to mean in the end – 7 **unqualified** total,
without reservation – 8 **approval** showing that one considers sth to be good – 9 **adolescence** [ˌdəˈlesns] period when one is changing from child to adult – 9 **inextricably**
[ˌɪnɪkˈstrɪkəbli] in a way impossible to separate – 11 **quasi** resembling to some degree –
12 **sanction** approval – 13 **to diffuse** to spread – 14 **Providence** God's protection – 15 **to
signify** to mean, show – 22 **to be insatiable for sth** [ɪnˈseɪʃəbl] to constantly require
more and never be able to get enough of sth – 24 **promissory note** written promise
to pay a certain sum of money – 25 **conspicuously** easily seen – 26 **to recur** to happen
repeatedly – 26 **stern** firm, strict – 26 **harsh** with no sympathy or kindness

This "rating" aspect of money is for Americans [...] at least as important as any of the uses to which it can be put. Of course the purchasing power of the dollar is important for securing the basic necessities of life (and these are variously defined); but
5 once these have been secured, its social value is at least as great as its purchasing power.

From *The American People – A Study in National Character* by Geoffrey Gorer, New York: W. W. Norton, 1948, pp. 106, 174-175. Reprinted by permission.

8. How to Get People to Like You

The fact is that popularity can be attained by a few simple, natural, normal, and easily mastered techniques. Practice them diligently and you can become a well-liked person. [...]
10 If you have gone through life up to this point without having established satisfactory human relationships, do not assume that you cannot change, but it will be necessary to take very definite steps toward solving the problem. You can change and become a popular person, well liked and esteemed, if you are
15 willing to make the effort. [...]
The basic principles of getting people to like you need no prolonged and labored emphasis, for they are very simple and easily illustrate their own truth. However, I list ten practical rules for getting the esteem of others. The soundness of these princi-
20 ples has been demonstrated innumerable times. Practice them until you become expert at them and people will like you.
1. Learn to remember names. Inefficiency at this point may indicate that your interest is not sufficiently outgoing. A man's name is very important to him.
25 2. Be a comfortable person so there is no strain in being with you – be an old-shoe, old-hat kind of individual. Be homey.

1 **to rate** to decide the value or position of sth,*here:* the social position – 3 **to secure** to get, obtain – 7 **to attain** to gain or achieve after making an effort – 8 **to master** to learn to do sth skillfully – 8 **technique** [tɛkˈniːk] particular method of doing sth – 9 **diligently** [ˈdɪlɪdʒəntli] carefully, with a great deal of effort – 14 **esteemed** admired and respected – 16 **prolonged** continuing for a long time – 17 **labored** requiring a lot of effort – 19 **soundness** correctness, reasonableness – 20 **innumerable** [ɪˈnuːmərəbl] so often that it can't be counted – 22 **inefficiency** [ˌɪnɪˈfɪʃnsi] not putting in the effort to succeed – 23 **outgoing** [–ˈ– –] sociable, open – 25 **strain** tension, stress – 26 **old-shoe, old-hat** comfortable to be with (like things you're used to) – 26 **homey** friendly, easy to be with

3. Acquire the quality of relaxed easy-goingness so that things do not ruffle you.

4. Don't be egotistical. Guard against giving the impression that you know it all. Be natural and normally humble.

5   5. Cultivate the quality of being interesting so that people will want to be with you and get something of stimulating value from their association with you.

6. Study to get the "scratchy" elements out of your personality, even those of which you may be unconscious.

10   7. Sincerely attempt to heal, on an honest Christian basis, every misunderstanding you have had or now have. Drain off your grievances.

8. Practice liking people until you learn to do so genuinely. Remember what Will Rogers said, "I never met a man I didn't
15   like." Try to be that way.

9. Never miss an opportunity to say a word of congratulation upon anyone's achievement, or express sympathy in sorrow or disappointment.

10. Get a deep spiritual experience so that you have some-
20 thing to give people that will help them to be stronger and meet life more effectively. Give strength to people and they will give affection to you.

9. Smile at Someone!

I have asked thousands of business men to smile at someone every hour of the day for a week and then come to class and talk
25 about the results. How has it worked? Let's see … Here is a letter from William B. Steinhardt, a member of the New York Curb Exchange. His case isn't isolated. In fact, it is typical of hundreds of others.

1 **to acquire** to get – 2 **to ruffle** to upset (usually: to be ruffled by) – 3 **to guard against doing sth** to be careful not to do sth – 4 **humble** modest, not too proud of oneself – 6 **to stimulate** to inspire, to cause enthusiasm – 8 **scratchy** rough, negative – 9 **unconscious** [ʌnˈkɒnʃəs] unaware – 10 **to heal** to set right, to make sth bad good again – 11 **to drain off** *here:* to gradually get rid of – 12 **grievance** cause for complaint or protest – 13 **genuinely** [ˈdʒenjʊɪnli] sincerely, truly – 14 **Will Rogers** (1879-1935) American humorist – 26 **New York Curb Exchange** stock exchange (Börse) that later became the American Stock Exchange

"I have been married for over eighteen years," writes Mr. Steinhardt, "and in all that time I seldom smiled at my wife or spoke two dozen words to her from the time I got up until I was ready to leave for business. I was one of the worst grouches who
5   ever walked down Broadway.

"Since you asked me to make a talk about my experience with smiles, I thought I would try it for a week. So the next morning, while combing my hair, I looked at my glum mug in the mirror and said to myself, 'Bill, you are going to wipe the scowl off that
10   sour puss of yours today. You are going to smile. And you are going to begin right now.' As I sat down to breakfast, I greeted my wife with a 'Good morning, my dear,' and smiled as I said it.

"You warned me that she might be surprised. Well, you under-
15   estimated her reaction. She was bewildered. She was shocked. I told her that in the future she could expect this as a regular occurrence and I have kept it up every morning now for two months.

"This changed attitude of mine has brought more happiness
20   in our home during these two months than there was during the last year. "As I leave for my office now, I greet the elevator boy in the apartment house with a 'Good Morning' and a smile. I greet the doorman with a smile.

I smile at the cashier in the subway booth when I ask for
25   change. As I stand on the floor on the Curb Exchange, I smile at men who never saw me smile until recently.

"I soon found that everybody was smiling back at me. I treat those who come to me with complaints or grievances in a cheerful manner. I smile as I listen to them and I find that
30   adjustments are accomplished much easier.

I find that smiles are bringing me dollars, many dollars every day.

---

4 **grouch** [graʊtʃ] person who complains all the time and is easily irritated – 8 **glum** gloomy, sad – 8 **mug** *(sl.)* face – 9 **to wipe off** *here:* to get rid of – 9 **scowl** [skaʊl] look of anger – 10 **sour** bad-tempered, unfriendly – 10 **puss** [ʊ] *(sl.)* face – 14 **to underes-timate sth** to judge sth to be less than it is – 15 **bewildered** [bɪˈwɪldəd] confused – 17 **occurrence** event, sth that happens – 17 **to keep sth up** to continue doing sth – 21 **elevator** lift*(B.E)* – 21 **elevator boy** man who operates an elevator – 22 **apartment house** block of flats*(B.E.)* – 24 **cashier** [kæˈʃɪə] person in a restaurant, department store, in charge of receiving money from customers – 24 **subway booth** kind of stand at the entrance of the New York City underground system where you can get the correct change for travelling on the subway train – 30 **adjustment** small but necessary change – 30 **to accomplish** to complete successfully

"I make my office with another broker. One of his clerks is a likable young chap, and I was so elated about the results I was getting that I told him recently about my new philosophy of human relations. He then confessed that when I first came to
5 make my office with his firm he thought me a terrible grouch – and only recently changed his mind. He said I was really human when I smiled.

"I have also eliminated criticism from my system. I give appreciation and praise now instead of condemnation. I have
10 stopped talking about what I want. I am now trying to see the other person's viewpoint. And these things have literally revolutionized my life. I am a totally different man, a happier man, a richer man, richer in friendships and happiness – the only things that matter much after all."

15 Remember this letter was written by a sophisticated, worldly-wise stockbroker who makes his living buying and selling stocks for his own account on the New York Curb Exchange – a business so difficult that 99 out of every 100 who attempt it fail.

20 You don't feel like smiling? Then what? Two things. First, force yourself to smile. If you are alone, force yourself to whistle or hum a tune or sing. Act as if you were already happy, and that will tend to make you happy.

Here is the way the late Professor William James of Harvard
25 put it:

"Action seems to follow feeling, but really action and feeling go together, and by regulating the action, which is under the more direct control of the will, we can indirectly regulate the feeling, which is not.

30 "Thus the sovereign voluntary path to cheerfulness, if our cheerfulness be lost, is to sit up cheerfully and to act and speak as if cheerfulness were already there . . ."

From *How to Win Friends and Influence People*, New York: Pocket Books, n.d., 115th printing, pp. 72-74. Copyright © 1936 by Dale Carnegie; copyright renewed © 1964 by Donna Dale Carnegie and Dorothy Carnegie. Reprinted by permission of Simon & Schuster, Inc.

1 **to make one's office with sb** to share an office with sb – 1 **broker, stockbroker** person who acts as an agent in the buying and selling of stocks (Aktien) – 2 **elated** joyful, extremely happy – 9 **condemnation** [– –ˈ– –] very strong criticism and disapproval – 11 **literally** really, truly – 15 **sophisticated** well-informed, experienced – 17 **for his own account** for himself, not for a firm or business – 22 **hum** to sing a tune without opening one's mouth – 24 **William James** (1842-1910) American philosopher – 30 **sovereign** ['sɒvrɪn] *here:* most effective, best – 30 **voluntary** done of one's own free will

10. "On a Smile and a Shoeshine"

What is important in [Dale Carnegie's] and the many other books and schools which promise social success and happiness is the implicit view of the personality, of the self. For the Americans who buy the books and join the schools we are not "as God
5 made us"; by taking thought we may not be able to add a cubit to our stature but we can change the figure we present to the world. The Personality is seen as something to be manipulated, almost as a raw material, Character as subordinate to Will.

Here, once again, the second generation is probably crucial.
10 The children of foreigners from every land, with every type of temperament and every physical constitution, were turned into Americans at school; personality need not be merely the product of inherited characteristics and the impact of experience; it need not be a slow growth which must be fostered; it can also
15 be manipulated and remolded nearer to the heart's desire, or at least to the type which will win friends and influence people, bring in the orders, put over a "commercial" smoothly, leave the customer contented.

The implications are many. The unsociable or eccentric per-
20 son is to be blamed, not pitied (at least outside New England); he could change his personality if he wanted to and tried hard enough; the fact that he has not done so shows either a weak will or more probably "orneriness" and contempt for the opinions of others. "You, too, can be popular . . ."
25 Personality is, as it were, a raw material to be developed and exploited, in a manner analogous to any other raw material; the enterprising and fortunately circumstanced can develop and exploit it for their own benefit; but many will perforce sell or lease their charm, their frankness, their warmth, their sexual

3 **implicit** without any doubt, unquestioning – 5 **by taking thought** by controlling our will – 5 **cubit** ['kjuːbɪt] a former unit of measurement (Elle) – 6 **stature** ['stɪ tʃə] height – 8 **subordinate** having a less important position – 9 **crucial** ['kruːʃl] very important – 11 **constitution** state of health – 13 **inherited** received from one's parents – 13 **impact** ['– –] effect – 14 **to foster sth** to help in the development of sth – 15 **to remold sth** to give a new shape to sth – 17 **orders** orders for goods – 17 **put over** to communicate successfully – 19 **implication** sth which is suggested but not directly mentioned – 20 **to blame sb** to hold sb responsible for (a wrong-doing) – 23 **orneriness** ['ɔːnərɪnəs] the quality of being stubborn, bad-tempered – 23 **contempt** lack of respect or regard – 25 **as it were** so to speak – 26 **to exploit** [–'–] to use sth as fully as possible, to use to one's own advantage – 26 **analogous to** [ə'nɪ ləgəs] similar, equivalent to – 27 **fortunately circumstanced** ['– – – –] wealthy – 28 **perforce** [–'–] necessarily – 29 **to lease** [liːs] **sth to sb** to let sb use sth in return for regular payments – 29 **frankness** openness, honesty

appeal, their voice, to an employer to exploit for his benefit in the same way as they will sell their labor. A winning smile or a pleasant voice is nearly as marketable a business commodity as a knowledge of accountancy or skill in mining. It is a curi-
5 ous comment on the change in values that "selling oneself" is a meritorious and praiseworthy act on the part of a young person setting out in life, and is a necessary preliminary to "selling" an idea or a project, and, in most cases, to acquiring a job. A person incapable of "selling" him or herself is badly handicapped.

From *The American People – A Study in National Character* by Geoffrey Gorer, New York: W. W. Norton, 1948, pp. 136-138. Reprinted by permission.

11. Tim Devlin – Ex-Salesman

10 *He suffered a nervous breakdown and was in the hospital for three months. He's been out for a year. "I'm thirty years old and I sometimes feel fifty." (Laughs)*

Right now I'm doing work that I detest. I'm a janitor. It's a dirty job. You work hard. When I'm at work I wear a uniform, gray
15 khaki pants and a gray shirt. It's baggy pants. It's what you see a lot of janitors wearing. This is the kind of work I used to think niggers would do or hillbillies or DPs. You don't associate with people like that. Now I'm one of them.

"You're a bum" – this is the picture I have of myself. I'm a flop
20 because of what I've come to. There's five of us at work here. It's a housing project.

Three can barely speak a word of English. They're DPs. They work very hard and don't complain. They're perfectly content, but I'm not. It's a dead end. Tonight I'm gonna meet a couple of
25 friends at a bar. I haven't seen them for a long time. I feel infe- rior. I'll bullshit 'em. I'll say I'm a lawyer or something.

---

3 **marketable** possible to sell – 3 **commodity** product – 4 **accountancy** [–́– – –] theory and practice of keeping financial records – 6 **meritorious** [ˌmerɪtɔːriəs] deserving reward, praise – 6 **on the part of a person** as far as that person is concerned – 7 **to set out** to begin – 7 **preliminary** [–́– – – –] sth that prepares for or introduces a main event or action – 9 **handicapped** at a disadvantage – 13 **to detest** to hate – 13 **jani- tor** [ˈdʒænɪtə] person who takes care of and cleans a large building – 15 **baggy** big and loose-fitting – 17 **hillbilly** person of the lower social classes, especially from the southeastern United States – 17 **DP** displaced person: person forced to leave his or her country because of war – 19 **flop** *(coll.)* failure – 21 **housing project** group of buildings built with government money for low-income families – 24 **dead end** sth with no future – 26 **lawyer** Rechtsanwalt

When you meet somebody at a party they ask, "What do you do?" I bullshit 'em. I tell 'em anything. Their minds are like a computer. "I'm a CPA." Oh, he's gotta make at least eighteen thousand a year. He's a success. If I said I was an electrician,
5   they'd think I make nine dollars an hour. If you say, "I'm a janitor" – ooohhh! You get this feeling that you are low. It's a blow to my ego. Who wants to be a janitor? They even call them maintenance engineers.

I don't have any interest in furthering myself, but I just can't
10 see myself doing this the rest of my life. I almost get to the point that I ought to be on welfare. I ought to chuck it all and just not do anything. My whole outlook on work is different than it was. I'd be free if I could say I'm a janitor … If I could only say, "I'm Tim Devlin and I enjoy what I'm doing!"

15 I've had college training and I'd been in sales almost eight years. I was right off the assembly line: In life you become a success to get ahead; money is the key to judge people by. That was my childhood thing – the big office, the big car, the big house. I was doing as good as I wanted to be. I could have done much
20 better.

I fell in love and thought it was the most beautiful experience in the world. Shortly after I was married I found out that my wife – I'm not blaming her – was interested in money. She was judging me against other people my age.

25 Was I a financial success? I put in long hours. I got this feeling I was just a machine. I felt at the end of the week. Here's the money. Now do you love me? Am I a better man? […]

I was one of their soldiers. I read the sales manuals. If the customer says this, you say that. Turn him around, get him in the
30 palm of your hand, and boom! – get him to sign on the dotted

---

3 **CPA** certified public accountant (Wirtschaftsprüfer) – 6 **a blow to one's ego** sth that makes one think less of oneself – 7 **maintenance** act of keeping things in good working condition – 9 **to further oneself** to advance oneself either academically or professionally – 11 **to be on welfare** to receive money from the state because of being unemployed, etc. – 11 **to chuck** *(coll.)* to throw (away), to give up – 12 **outlook** way of looking at sth – 15 **to be in sales** to work as a salesperson – 16 **assembly line** Fließband – 16 **I was right off the assembly line** I was a typical mass product of the system – 17 **to get ahead** to do better than others – 25 **to put in** to work – 28 **manual** ['mɒnjuəl] small book of instructions – 29 **to get sb in the palm of your hand** to get full control and influence over sb – 30 **palm** [pɑːm] the inside of one's hand excluding the finger – 30 **boom** word to describe a sudden sound or movement – 30 **dotted line** line made up of a series of dots at the bottom of a contract where you sign your name

line. You give him bullshit. You wiggle, you finagle, you sell yourself, and you get him to sign. Pow! you won a round. The next
day is another round. What the hell am I doing? I don't enjoy it.
My marriage is turning sour. I'm making good money. I have a
5 company car. This is what my wife wants, but I feel bad. I begin
to question things. It blew the whole marriage.

I never talk about it to anyone. People would think I'm a
communist or I'm going crazy. A person that's making money
shouldn't question the source of it. I always kept it to myself.
10 This was the American Dream. [...] We should examine this
dream. If I sell a machine that's worth $480 for $1,250, is that
the American Dream? [...]

I do want to make it financially. But the only thing open for
me would be sales work again. I'm not twenty-one any more.
15 My God, I'd have to start off with maybe a hundred and a quar-
ter a week. That really isn't any money. That's just enough to
put a roof over your head. If I do apple polishing, I might make
assistant manager in ten years – and maybe a lot of titles along
the way. I'm afraid that's the only way open for me now. I guess I
20 could buy stock, get remarried, and be part of what the system's
all about. But I really question the system ...

From *Working: People Talk About What They Do All Day and How They
Feel About Mat They Do* by Studs Terkel, New York: Avon Books, 1975,
pp. 340-343. Copyright © 1972, 1974 by Studs Terkel. Reprinted by
permission of Pantheon Books, a Division of Random House, Inc., New
York.

1 **to wiggle** *here:* to use clever and dishonest arguments – 1 **to finagle** [fi'neɪɡl] to trick,
to deceive – 2 **pow** boom – 4 **to turn sour** to turn bad – 6 **to blow** to destroy, to ruin –
17 **to do apple polishing** to do and say nice things to the boss in order to get a better
position – 17 **to make** *here:* to achieve the position of – 20 **stock** goods to sell

Glossary of Dramatic Terms

allusion An indirect but meaningful reference to a person, place, event, or literary work.

antagonist The character opposing the protagonist in a drama.

apron See forestage.

aside A short comment made by a character to the audience or another character that is not heard by the other characters on the stage.

backdrop A large piece of cloth painted with a scene hung at the back of the stage.

climax Often considered the same as the turning point: the point at which the main conflict becomes the most intense making the outcome of the conflict clear.

comedy A literary work – usually a drama – that is humorous in its treatment of theme and character and has a happy ending.

comic relief A short comic scene, usually in a tragedy, that for a moment reduces the tension.

dénouement The part of the plot where the final outcome of a conflict or complication is made known.

diction The choice and use of words in speech or writing.

downstage The front part of the stage.

dramatic irony Words spoken by a character that have for the audience a meaning not intended or even understood by the speaker.

flashback A scene inserted in a play or story that interrupts the logical sequence of time to relate something that happened at an earlier time.

foil A character that is used to contrast with another character.

foreshadowing Any hints or clues that indicate what will happen later.

forestage The part of the stage in front of the curtain.

inflection A change in the tone or loudness of the voice while speaking.

leitmotif In music: a recurring melody often associated with a certain character or mood. In a literary work: any recurring theme.

linear plot The plot that develops strictly along a chronological line.

offstage Occurring behind or next to the stage (e.g. sounds heard by the audience when the action that produces them cannot be seen).

plot The sequence of interrelated events taking place in a story or drama.

prop Any article such as a telephone, chair, etc. used as a part of the scenery on the stage.

protagonist The main character, hero.

reported action Events not occurring on stage but revealed from what the characters say.

represented action The action actually taking place on the stage.

retrospection The act of talking about events that took place in the past.

setting Time and place in which the events of a literary work take place.

soliloquy Speech delivered by a character alone on the stage, often revealing his innermost thoughts to the audience.

sound effects Sounds that are created artificially such as a door bell, a telephone ringing, thunder, etc.

stage directions A description of a character or the setting, or directions for the actor included in the text of the play.

stage set Props and scenery set up and arranged for a particular scene.

tragedy In classical drama: the destruction of a person of high birth often because of forces beyond his control. In modern drama: any play that arouses our pity, usually having "the common man" as the protagonist.

tragic flaw A weakness in the hero's character that causes his tragic downfall.

upstage The rear of the stage.